Ideology and Imagination

IDEOLOGY AND IMAGINATION

The Image of Society in Dostoevsky

GEOFFREY C. KABAT

NEW YORK   COLUMBIA UNIVERSITY PRESS   1978

The Andrew W. Mellon Foundation, through a special grant,
has assisted the Press in publishing this volume.

COLUMBIA UNIVERSITY PRESS
NEW YORK   GUILDFORD, SURREY

COPYRIGHT © 1978 COLUMBIA UNIVERSITY PRESS
ALL RIGHTS RESERVED.

PRINTED IN THE UNITED STATES OF AMERICA

LIBRARY OF CONGRESS CATALOGING IN PUBLICATION DATA
KABAT, GEOFFREY C
   IDEOLOGY AND IMAGINATION.
   BIBLIOGRAPHY: P.
   INCLUDES INDEX.
   1. DOSTOEVSKIĬ, FEDOR MIKHAĬLOVICH, 1821–1881—
POLITICAL AND SOCIAL VIEWS.   I. TITLE.
PG3328.Z7P66   891.7'3'3   78–9437
ISBN 0–231–04422–4

To My Parents

CONTENTS

PREFACE   ix

1 THE EMANCIPATION AND THE INTELLIGENTSIA   1

2 PERIOD OF TRANSITION: DOSTOEVSKY'S VIEW OF
   HISTORY   9

3 THE IMAGINATION OF SOCIETY   53

4 THE ECONOMICS OF WRITING   93

5 FANTASY AND FICTION   111

6 CREATIVE PROCESS: FROM IDEOLOGY TO
   IMAGINATION   163

   NOTES   181

   BIBLIOGRAPHY   193

   INDEX   199

PREFACE

THIS IS a study of Dostoevsky's views on Russian history and society and of the implications of these views for his writings between 1860 and 1881. Put differently, it is a study of the relations between Dostoevsky's world view, his political ideology, and his literary imagination. I have taken Dostoevsky's view of history, or world view,[1] as a privileged starting point for understanding his later writings—his journalism, letters, and fiction—as a whole. By world view, I mean a set of attitudes toward and questions about Russia's historical situation which underlie all Dostoevsky's writings. These attitudes and questions were unsettling, and they reflected a deep anxiety within the Russian intelligentsia. But they were also, I would like to suggest, creative—especially in the case of Dostoevsky; that is, they called out for solutions.

The world view poses problems, contradictions, which Dostoevsky attempted to resolve in his various writings. Central to Dostoevsky's world view are certain oppositions—between Russia and Europe; between the peasantry and the educated class in Russia; between Russia's past and her future—and certain questions: How can Russia avoid repeating the experience of Western Europe with its class struggles and warring nationalisms? How is Russia to overcome her division into two classes and her alienation from herself? What is it that binds a society together and gives people a sense of identity, of a foundation, of a connection with one another? All Dostoevsky's writings are concerned with these and related questions, and his journalism, letters, and fiction can be seen as responses to them in different modes.

Dostoevsky's view of history is expressed at greatest length in his journalism: his articles for his journals *Vremja* (1861–63) and *Epokha* (1864–65), his unpublished drafts of articles (written during the 1860s and 1870s and now published under the title *The Unpublished Dostoevsky*), and, finally, *The Diary of a Writer* from 1873, 1876–77, 1880, and 1881. Together these writings offer a comprehensive picture of his views during the last twenty years of his life and allow one to conclude that Dostoevsky's views on history, Russian society, and Russia's relation to Europe remained remarkably stable throughout this period, despite shifts in his political attitudes. By the early 1860s, the main lines and themes of his world view were formed. For this reason, I have drawn on all of Dostoevsky's journalistic writings in my exposition of his world view (chapter 2) without regard for chronology and have treated the more abundant later material of *The Diary of a Writer* as an elaboration of themes and ideas which are present in the articles of the early 1860s.

There are several reasons for approaching Dostoevsky's writings by way of his journalism. First, Dostoevsky was very much rooted in his time, in a specific period of history, and he was deeply preoccupied with events taking place both in Russia and in Europe. The journalism copiously reflects this preoccupation and brings into the foreground questions present, if not explicit, in all Dostoevsky's writings.

Second, the journalism and the world view that emerges from it allow us to see Dostoevsky in relation to his contemporaries. Dostoevsky was a member of a distinct social group—the intelligentsia—which he addresses in his writings, and he shared fundamental concerns with particular segments of the intelligentsia—specifically, with the Russian populists—even though he was at odds with them over questions of principle. Dostoevsky's journalism is, among other things, a protracted commentary on the position of the intelligentsia in Russian society, and through his meditation on society he defines his own position in it.

Finally, when Dostoevsky's writings are seen as responses

to the contradictions and dilemmas pointed up by his world view, both the unity and the complexity of his thought become more intelligible. In grappling with the dilemmas inherent in his world view, Dostoevsky manifests two radically different styles of thought which are tied to two different sides of his personality. These two styles of thought which I call the *ideological* and the *imaginative* are often closely intertwined, but, broadly speaking, the ideological mode is dominant in the journalism and the imaginative mode is dominant in the fiction.[2] The ideological mode represents an attempt to overcome a contradiction by means of aggressive self-assertion and denial of the other. It resolves conflicting terms into absolutes ("we" versus "they"; "Russia" versus "Europe"; present versus future) between which no mediation is possible. The only way to overcome a contradiction between two terms in this mode is by the inflation and aggrandizement of one of the terms to the point where it swallows up or overrules the other. This attitude—this thirst for immediate and total transformations of self and society, this urge to eliminate all contradictions—is most evident in Dostoevsky's nationalism (his fantasies about Russia's absorbing Constantinople and Central Asia), his anti-Semitism, and his xenophobia. It is also expressed on a personal level in Dostoevsky's compulsive gambling, which he sees as a means of overcoming oppositions, of changing his life by one decisive act. In the fiction, this attitude inhabits those major characters who attempt to overcome oppositions by instantaneous acts. But, in representing the ideological mode in the fiction, Dostoevsky transcends it and dissociates himself from it.

In the imaginative mode, Dostoevsky is free to explore the deeper connections between the terms of a contradiction and to mediate between contraries. The terms of a contradiction are no longer seen as absolutes but as functions of a larger (social) context in which they are embedded. In the fiction, Dostoevsky shows that the way to overcome contradictions is to reveal what gives rise to them. Ideology, which is an inadequate attempt at mediation and is seen as such in the fiction, yields to an authentic form of mediation through writing which uncovers hidden connections between apparently unrelated phenomena and which comes to accept and integrate that which is foreign and disturbing.

Thus, Dostoevsky's fiction is the furthest exploration of the dilemmas raised by his world view. Rather than programs or formulas, rather than immediate change, it offers an alternative view of reality based on an image of totality, community, interconnectedness.

This study began as a doctoral dissertation submitted at Columbia University. I am greatly indebted to Grigory A. Byaly of Leningrad State University, who helped me in my early research during an eight-month stay in the Soviet Union, and to Robert Belknap, Rufus Mathewson, Jr., and William Harkins, who read the original manuscript and made many helpful suggestions. Other colleagues and friends read—and in many cases, reread—the manuscript at various stages of its evolution and offered thoughtful comments, enthusiasm, and encouragement. In particular, I want to thank James T. Clifford, David Parmacek, David Halle, Joan Spivak, Daniel Serwer, John Hoberman, Joseph Frank, and Richard Wertime. Finally, I am grateful to Karen Mitchell of Columbia University Press for her careful editing of the manuscript.

Ideology and Imagination

1

THE EMANCIPATION
AND THE INTELLIGENTSIA

Look! The fire of "economic progress" has already reached the roots of our
national life. Under its influence the old forms of social life are being razed.
The very "principle of the commune"—the principle which is the cornerstone
of that future social order which we all dream of, is being destroyed. Amid the
ruins of consumed forms, new forms are being born. Exploitation and preda-
toriness [kulachestvo, miroedstvo] develop; the principle of individualism, of
economic anarchy, of heartless, avid egoism installs itself.
                                                    —P. N. Tkachev (1875)[1]

In December, 1859 Dostoevsky, aged thirty eight, returned to
Petersburg to resume his literary career almost ten years to
the day after being sent to Siberia in chains for his participation in a tiny radical group devoted to the discussion of utopian socialism.[2] During his years of imprisonment and exile,
momentous changes had taken place in Russian society, and
even greater changes were anticipated. Dostoevsky's return to
the capital coincided with the high point in the controversy
surrounding the impending emancipation of the serfs.

Three events in particular had signaled the approaching
transformation of Russian society. First, the stultifying thirty-
year regime of Nicholas I had come to an end in 1855, and
the succession of his son Alexander II quickened hopes
among both the peasantry and the intelligentsia that their
situations would improve. Second, Russia's defeat in the Cri-

mean War had forced her to acknowledge her military and technological backwardness in comparison with Europe, and this new awareness led to a policy of modernization. Third, soon after the end of the war, the new Tsar bade the gentry propose steps for freeing the serfs, and by the fall of 1858 provincial committees had been established throughout Russia. (Until 1857 the censorship had not allowed the slightest public discussion of serfdom as a policy issue.) Taken together, these three events seemed to point to a determination to transform Russia from a primitive empire into a modern European state, and the years preceding the emancipation were a time of unprecedented optimism.

When it finally came, however, the emancipation proved a disappointment to almost all the parties concerned. The settlement, which was the result of nearly five years of deliberations on the part of the bureaucracy, with the consultation of the conservative gentry and the liberal gentry, was embodied in a 300-page document of bewildering complexity and obscurity. Although the liberal gentry had exerted a strong influence during the first few years of debates, in the end the conservative gentry managed to obstruct any radical change. The emancipation was at best half-hearted and hedged with restrictions. At worst—and this was the view of the radical intelligentsia and of the peasantry, insofar as one can tell—it was a fraud.

The serfs received personal freedom and could no longer be sold or transferred against their will. And they were allotted land, against the wishes of the more conservative gentry. But the granting of personal freedom did not mean that the peasants obtained the same civil rights as the gentry. Rather, they were tied, in most regions, to the village commune, which was responsible for the collection of taxes, including the redemption payments for the land they received. Furthermore, and contrary to the peasants' expectations, they had to pay for their land and "at a price so high that it in fact included a redemption of [their] person also."[3] The redemption process itself, by which the peasants paid back the state for their land (the state having compensated the landowners for the loss of their serfs), was preceded by a "temporary obligation period" of unspecified duration during which the peasants could not refuse their allotments and had to perform obligations on them. This meant that for a period of several years following the emancipation, little in fact changed in the peasants' situation. Most important was the fact that when they finally were freed, the peasants were not given enough land to subsist on. They received only that land which had been in their possession under the serf system and which required only half their labor (since they worked half the week for the landowner).[4]

Owing to the inadequacy of the allotments, to the enforced immobility of the peasants, and to the rapidly increasing rural population, a general land hunger developed among the peasantry as a result of the emancipation.[5] More and more peasants were forced to take up supplementary occupations as craftsmen or industrial workers or to lease additional lands at high rents in order to meet their obligations to their former masters, to pay their taxes, and to support themselves.[6] Some historians have concluded that the condition of the peasantry following the emancipation was generally worse than before it and that their situation continued to decline throughout the last four decades of the nineteenth century.[7] The full extent of the peasants' disappointment with the emancipation revealed itself in the disturbances that followed its proclamation and in the persistent rumors that the Tsar's will had been perverted by the landowners and the bureaucrats and that once the Tsar learned of the deception, he would grant the peasants "true freedom."[8]

As for its effect on the gentry, Terence Emmons writes: "The emancipation dealt the gentry class an economic blow from which it never recovered."[9] The emancipation brought with it a settlement of the gentry's long-standing debts to the state, which left the gentry with little capital to invest in farming based on hired labor. "The gentry thus turned to renting the lands left them, and increasingly to selling them—an alternative which became progressively more attractive as land prices rose (under pressure of peasant land-hunger) but grain prices declined throughout the last third of the nineteenth century."[10] Thus, the emancipation seems to have adversely affected the two major classes of pre-1861 Russia—the peasantry and the landed gentry.

Paradoxically, in spite of its half-hearted and basically conservative nature, the emancipation indirectly gave a powerful impetus to the development of capitalism in Russia. Zaionchkovsky cites the "differentiation of the peasantry, i.e. its gradual disintegration into a bourgeoisie and a proletariat"; the "industrial revolution" which reached its peak at the end of the seventies; and the increase in internal trade as evidence of the development of capitalism in the post-reform period.[11] In the twenty years following the emancipation, the number of miles of railroad track increased from 1,000 to more than 14,000, and this expansion in turn provided a market for Russian heavy industry. Iron and coal production underwent rapid growth, as did the oil industry, cotton spinning, and woolen manufactures.[12] Grain exports rose dramatically from 69 million *poods* in the period 1856–60 to 120 million in 1866–70 and to 257 million in 1876–80.[13] This economic growth was accompanied by a rise in land prices, an increase in the number of hired laborers, and an expansion of the money economy.

In sum, the post-reform period was one of deep contradictions and ambiguities. Remnants of the traditional agrarian institutions were preserved side by side with the expansion of capitalism and the money economy. The future of the newly freed peasant was highly uncertain, as was that of the landowners. The peasant commune which the Slavophiles and the precursors of Russian populism—Herzen and Chernyshevsky—had looked to as the embodiment of a stable communal society appeared after the emancipation in the dual guise of a bulwark against the development of capitalism and the bureaucracy's instrument for the perpetuation of serfdom. Perhaps the major contradiction of this period—one which preoccupied both Dostoevsky and the populists—was that in order to modernize, the country had to go through a period of "primitive accumulation": it had to finance its budget at the expense of the newly liberated peasantry. As Lionel Kochan describes this situation:

emancipation dues and other taxes produced a steadily increasing peasant indebtedness. It was this, in fact that enabled Russia to maintain a consistently favorable balance of trade, to service all its foreign debt in the second half of the nineteenth century, and to maintain a strong rouble backed by gold. In order to pay his debts, the peasant had to sell his grain for export to Western Europe. But 'the granary of Europe' achieved its position only at the price of impoverishing its own population. The economic pressure was such that the peasant had to sell the grain that he actually needed for his own consumption. Chronic undernourishment in the Russian village was emphasized by the disproportionate effects of crop failure and, even more, by the increased mortality rate—from twenty-four to twenty-seven per thousand at the beginning of the nineteenth century to thirty-five per thousand in 1880.

By and large, the Russian masses completely failed to participate in the rise of the popular standard of living that elsewhere characterized the latter part of the nineteenth century. On the contrary, the acquisition of some degree of personal freedom was accompanied by a decline in living-standards, by land hunger, and by rural over-population.[14]

February 19, 1861, the date of the promulgation of the emancipation statutes, became a landmark in Russian history not only for its direct material consequences but also for its symbolic and psychological significance—for the hopes it aroused and failed to satisfy and for the anxieties it inspired about Russia's future. Whatever its immediate effects on the lives of the peasantry and the gentry, the emancipation marked a shift from serfdom to capitalism, from a bound-labor economy to a free-labor market economy. The elimination of the serf system and the granting of personal freedom to the peasants ushered in a series of reforms—administrative, educational, military, judicial—that the government had decided were urgently needed. Almost all contemporary observers agreed that the emancipation signaled a fundamental shift in Russian history which would have far-reaching consequences (although they did not necessarily agree on what those consequences would be). They saw it as heralding the emergence of a new organization of Russian society. For Dostoevsky, the emancipation was an event of critical significance that raised pressing and disquieting questions about Russia's future.

Confronted by Russia's situation in the post-reform period, the Russian intelligentsia, which had eagerly looked forward to the emancipation, feared that the forces of capitalist development unleashed by the emancipation would lead Russia on the same course as that they saw epitomized in Europe and especially in England. There, the peasantry had been forced off the land and into the factories, where they were reduced to wage slaves earning barely enough to keep them alive and working. The prospect of Russia's having to undergo a similar evolution dominated the thinking of much of the Russian intelligentsia in the 1860s and 1870s, especially the populists, [15] who, as a group, gave the most pointed formulation to the contradictions of Russia's situation. Social thinkers and critics like Mikhailovsky, Tkachev, Flerovsky, Bakunin, and Lavrov asserted that, owing to her economic backwardness, Russia could, if she acted in time, avoid Europe's disastrous experience and skip the capitalist phase of development. They maintained that by relying on her indigenous peasant institutions (above all, the village commune), Russia could evolve directly into a cooperative socialist society. These writers saw clearly the inadequacy of the emancipation: that it left the peasants worse off than they had been before and that it encouraged social differentiation within the peasantry and the formation of a strong bourgeoisie. It was these developments that they hoped to prevent at all costs. This awareness of Russia's potential to evolve a humane society and the simultaneous awareness of the foreclosing of this possibility account, to a great extent, for the tone of urgency in the writings of the populists and those of Dostoevsky.

The outlook of the populists, as Andrzej Walicki has argued, constitutes a coherent world view and has the "essential unity of a socially determined Weltanschauung."[16] "What united these very different men and very different movements was a certain body of ideas, certain attitudes towards capitalism, as opposed to the archaic structures of Russian social life."[17] Populism, in this sense, reflected the standpoint of "small producers (mainly peasants), willing to get rid of the remnants of serfdom, but, at the same time, endangered by the development of capitalism."[18] But in addition to being "an ideological reaction to the development of capitalism *inside Russia*," populism was also "a reaction to the capitalist economy and socialist thought of the West. It reflected *not only* the problems of the small producers in confrontation with large-scale capitalist production; it reflected *also* specific problems of a backward peasant country in confrontation with the highly developed capitalist states."[19]

Walicki lists the hallmarks of populism as follows: the desire to avoid capitalist development along with an emphasis on the peasant commune and the possibility of a direct transition to socialism; an emphasis on the price of capitalist development (here Walicki points to the influence of Marx's *Capital*); a critique of the mechanistic view of social development; an emphasis on the uniqueness of the Russian situation and its special promise; a belief in the possibility of learning from the experience of the West.

Although Dostoevsky never thought of himself as a populist, and at times found himself at odds with particular populists, it is striking how closely Dostoevsky conforms to

the hallmarks that Walicki has isolated as the core of populism.[20] It is a central assumption of this study that he shared a
common perspective with the populists—though he also held
other beliefs which were beyond the scope of populism and
even in conflict with it—and that this perspective had a profound effect on his thinking and writing in the last twenty
years of his life. Certain fundamental themes, concerns, and
paradoxes of Dostoevsky's work can best be understood in
the context of the populist world view.[21] Dostoevsky wrote
with an acute awareness of the pressing contradictions of Russian society in the post-reform period as well as an awareness
of those who were offering remedies for Russia's dilemma.
Among the latter, the populists were undoubtedly the most
vigorous and the most incisive in the 1860s and 1870s. Dostoevsky's complex social thought can be seen as the product
of the play between sympathy and identification with the critics of Russian society *and* a criticism of the shortcomings and
excesses of the critics themselves. His fiction derives much of
its complexity and richness from the double perspective that
he adopted. He presents both a critique of society and, at the
same time, a critique of the current ideas and programs of
those who would change society. By dramatizing Russia's dilemma, largely in populist terms, and by dramatizing the limitations of populist solutions and theories, Dostoevsky was, in
a sense, exhausting the possibilities of the present and demonstrating the need for a new way of thinking about Russian
society.

2

PERIOD OF TRANSITION: DOSTOEVSKY'S VIEW OF HISTORY

I do not want to think and live any other way than with the belief that all our ninety million Russians, or however many of them there will be then, will be educated and civilized, humanized and happy. That light and the higher blessings of life are bestowed only on 1/10, according to Potugin's civilization. With this condition of only 1/10 of the people being happy, I would not want civilization then. I (want) believe [sic] in the complete Kingdom of Christ. How it will be done, it is difficult to foresee, but it will be. I believe that this kingdom will come. But even though it is difficult to foresee, signs in the dark night of conjecture can still be envisioned mentally and I believe in these signs. And the universal kingdom of thought and light will come to pass, and it will be here in Russia perhaps sooner than anywhere else.[1]

THROUGHOUT the latter part of his life, Dostoevsky shared with the Russian populists the belief that Russia stood at a decisive turning point in its history, that it was necessary for Russia to break with its past and to realize its unique historical and cultural identity in order to avoid recapitulating the historical evolution of Western Europe. He found confirmation for his belief in the emancipation of the serfs, which he enthusiastically attributed solely to the magnanimity of Alexander II, rather than to a variety of practical considerations and interests. Dostoevsky hails the emancipation as the end of a two-hundred-year period of national alienation and internal division—dating from the time of Peter the Great—and as the prelude to a new period of Russian history that would see the uniting of the peasantry and the gentry, who had been isolated from one another by serfdom. Although the emancipation marked a formal end to what Dostoevsky calls Russia's "Petersburg period," the contradictions which defined that period persist even after the emancipation, and Dostoevsky sees their resolution as Russia's most pressing task. Dostoevsky characterizes the post-reform period—in which he wrote his most important works and about which he wrote—as an interim period, a time of transition, in which the old order (serfdom) has come to an end and in which the outlines of a new order are not yet distinguishable.

Dostoevsky acknowledges that the emancipation, rather than bringing about the desired change in Russian society, has aggravated its ills: "Strangely, the dark moral aspects of the old order—egotism, cynicism, slavery, disunity, and venality—not only have not disappeared with the abolition of serfdom but have, as it were, grown stronger, more developed, more numerous" (*The Diary of a Writer*, p. 107).[2] "The economic and moral condition of the people after the abolition of serfdom is awful. Irrefutable and most disturbing facts attest to this every minute" (*Diary*, p. 30). He describes the post-emancipation period as one of chaos, obscurity, fragmentation, and loss of traditional values. The present for him is a time of paradox, of conflict, of total lack of consensus in Russian society. He comments that Russians in general display an urge for negation and self-destruction, an urge for the abyss (*Diary*, p. 40), and that "the people have become affected with an unheard of distortion of ideas and a wholesale worship of materialism" (*Diary*, p. 187).

Poised in the interim period following the emancipation, in which remnants of the old order persist alongside new forces which are making themselves felt, Dostoevsky looks ahead to the overcoming of the divisions of the Petersburg period and tries to discern the features of a unified, autonomous, self-assured Russia. His awareness of being in limbo, between a past which has not quite ended and a future which has not quite begun, is no doubt responsible for the basic tension that runs through all his writings of this period: between a chaotic, unsatisfactory, often intolerable, present and an imagined harmonious future; between a fragmented identity and a full, strong identity—both national and individual. This tension is at the heart of Dostoevsky's world view, his view of history, which in turn underlies all of his writings. In all of his writings, Dostoevsky is attempting to reconcile the oppositions of the Petersburg period and thereby to mediate between the chaotic present and a harmonious future, to establish continuity, at least in thought, between what appear as radically discontinuous states. The passage from Dostoevsky's notebook quoted as the epigraph to this chapter articulates the painful situation of the observer who longs for a society in which all would be included, in which division would no longer exist. Dostoevsky expresses the difficulty of conceiving of the transition from present to future; but he also asserts his faith that this transition will be achieved. In this state of tension, of being-in-between, of suspense, of waiting, of trying to make out the filiations between present and future, the writer grasps at "signs in the dark night of conjecture." Throughout *The Diary of a Writer* and his other journalism, Dostoevsky examines the signs, the facts of the present, in order to grasp the outlines of a desired future order. Writing for him is the work of mediating between the present and future, the real and the ideal, the painful, discordant, threatening external world and an inner vision of harmony.

His efforts to mediate take different forms in his journalism, letters, and fiction. In *The Diary*, the tension between present and future seems to call forth two alternating responses in Dostoevsky: the abstract assertion of Russia's inevitable future mission, and attention to the raw facts of the present in order to understand the causes of current phenomena. On the one hand, Dostoevsky holds to the idea of Russia's special future mission, the grandiose dialectic whereby she will attain her full stature and recognition among European nations. This attitude in its extreme form is based on the assertion of an inevitable line of historical development. It maintains that Russia is essentially different from all other nations and that Russia's mission is to resolve the conflicts that afflict the corrupted, moribund European nations. It makes a radical separation between present and future, and focuses on a future which will redeem the present situation. This attitude, which I call *ideological*, is, as I shall argue in the last chapter, both a form of defense and an attempt to establish by fiat a desired state of affairs. It finds its ultimate expression in Dostoevsky's militant nationalism, his pan-Slavism, his xenophobia, and his anti-Semitism. On the other hand, throughout *The Diary*, Dostoevsky is obsessed with the minute particulars of history, with lived history, and cannot sit back and watch the dialectic work itself out. His references to Russia's future mission and her preeminence among other nations are largely exhortatory. The future which he delineates is in the realm of the possible, but he knows that it will not be accomplished mechanically, that there is no law of history working itself out independent of man.

Fundamental to Dostoevsky's concern with history is the sustained character of his perception of crisis both in Russia and in the West. Dostoevsky, apparently, could not content himself with the arid ideological formulas which he never tired of preaching. It was not sufficient to predict the course of European civilization or of Russia; he had constantly to evaluate the forces which would contribute to either the realization or the undermining of his desideratum, to seek confirmation or disconfirmation of his predictions *in the present*. This second attitude, which I call *imaginative*, is an attempt to see the future evolving out of the present, rather than to conjure away an unpleasant reality in the name of a posited future. There is, then, in *The Diary* a tension not only between the empirical present and the desired future, but also between two attitudes: one characterized by abstract, ideological pronouncements about history and the other characterized by attention to the raw, daily facts of lived history. I will return to this distinction later in this chapter in discussing Dostoevsky's nationalism and again in the last chapter. But for the present we must turn to the view of history that calls forth these two different responses.

Dostoevsky locates the source of Russia's existing state of confusion and division (as well as of her future mission) in the reforms of Peter the Great at the beginning of the eighteenth century. Peter's opening up of Russia to Europe is, for Dostoevsky, unquestionably the most decisive event in Russian history, and, as we have seen, the legacy of the Petersburg period still dominates post-emancipation Russia. One is tempted to say that Peter's reforms represent for Dostoevsky Russia's fall into history, into striving and differentiation. The pre-Petrine Muscovite state appeared to both Slavophiles and Westerners of the nineteenth century as a self-contained, static, essentially timeless empire. Contact with Europe not only ushered Russia onto the stage of history but also changed her relation to herself. After Peter, Russia could no longer view herself unselfconsciously. The fall into history is necessarily a fall into self-consciousness (as it was for Hegel). It seems that the question of Russia's destiny could hardly have been posed before she came to see herself face to face with another culture so different and so much more advanced than her own. Throughout the Petersburg period, the opposition of Russia to Europe remained a central fact of Russian consciousness[3]—Russia constantly measured herself against the standard of Europe—and, as we will see, this opposition provides a backdrop for all of Dostoevsky's later writings.

In Dostoevsky's historical schema, the opposition Russia-Europe appears to be the source of further oppositions within Russian society which characterize the Petersburg period and which preoccupy Dostoevsky. In response to the encounter with European science and culture, Russian society became split into an educated minority which absorbed and prided itself on this new culture and the Russian masses which remained untouched by it. Furthermore, the intelligentsia, when it became aware of the problem of the masses and of Russia's destiny in relation to Europe, split into Slavophiles and Westerners. The people, too, are showing signs of becoming differentiated into rich peasants (kulaks) and poor ones. (Differentiation takes place not only along social lines but also between generations—between fathers and sons.) Thus, the primary opposition of Russia-Europe engenders new successive oppositions and divisions within Russian society. For Dostoevsky, contact with Europe is the origin of a line of development which has led to Russia's present state of social division and uncertainty over the future, but which also opens up the possibility of a higher stage of historical development.

In Dostoevsky's view, the separation of the gentry from the people, brought about by Peter, involved more than the adoption by the gentry of European values, more than just a cultural estrangement. A crucial element in Dostoevsky's characterization of the Petersburg period is his linking of Russia's division into two classes with the imposition of serfdom and the granting of privileges to the gentry in return for service to the state (which occurred under Peter). This link gives a specific historical content to Dostoevsky's preoccupation with the alienation of the intelligentsia, its detachment from the "soil," and its Europeanization—the dominant themes of the doctrine of pochvennichestvo,[4] which he formulated in the early 1860s and adhered to till the end of his life. It makes explicit the causal connection between the enslavement of the peasantry and the intelligentsia's acquisition of European culture, and it brings Dostoevsky closer to those populists, like Mikhailovsky and Lavrov, who emphasized the gentry's "debt to the people," the fact that the intelligentsia's culture was acquired at the expense of the people:

You [the intelligentsia] are constituting, as it were, an upper stratum above the people enveloping Russia; and according to your own statements and writings, it was for you that the Reformer left the people in servitude in order that by serving you with their labor, they might enable you to acquire European enlightenment. [*Diary*, p. 1028]

. . . forgetting the fact that this enlightenment was bought two centuries ago at the expense of serfdom and a Calvary of the Russian people serving us. [*Diary*, p. 1032]

Peter, whom Dostoevsky identifies with Russia's Europeanization, is also responsible for serfdom:

and you know what, the system of serf-ownership was really the veritable golden heritage of Peter's reform; it corresponded entirely to its spirit, and was its principal fruit.[5]

Thus, the intelligentsia's turn toward Europe meant not only the abandonment of the peasantry but the actual enslavement of the peasantry. The general alienation of the Petersburg period which Dostoevsky decries is not merely a spiritual matter. It is based on the active *alienating* of the peasantry, their subjection by the gentry and the state. This explicit link between Peter the Great and the imposition of serfdom, which is easily overlooked in Dostoevsky's writings, adds weight to Dostoevsky's world view and strengthens its claim to be taken as a serious, coherent view of history rather than as a mystical, historiosophical system.

The alienation of the Russian intelligentsia is the central theme of Dostoevsky's journalism and of *The Diary of a Writer* in particular. Insofar as the intelligentsia gives conscious expression to the national identity and insofar as it is the governing class, Russia's identity has become confused, distorted, dependent on Europe. The dilemma of the intelligentsia consists in its being unable to become either European or Russian—that is, one with the people. The intelligentsia is suspended between the opposed poles of Europe and the people. It is characterized by its negativity (except for one crucial asset—its culture—to which I will return later).

Dostoevsky describes the intelligentsia as having lost the habit of work, its native language, and a sense of the meaning of life, and as lacking any moral inheritance to pass on to future generations. The intelligentsia has been systematically emptied of substance during its period of European tutelage. It is this legacy of two hundred years of alienation that Dostoevsky is attempting in *The Diary* to bring to the attention of the intelligentsia and to reverse. He implies that the historic conditions responsible for this alienation have come to an end with the emancipation and that it is sufficient for the intelligentsia to become aware of its situation in order to change it.

As a result of Peter's turn to Europe, Dostoevsky maintains, the Russian educated elite became infatuated with European culture and ideas. Russians absorbed the Enlightenment, German Romanticism and Idealism, French utopian socialism, positivism, and utilitarianism and lived these intellectual currents with an intensity which owed a great deal to their foreignness. Dostoevsky regards educated Russians' infatuation with everything European as a form of snobbery— a pathetic attempt to be something other than what they are. As early as 1847 in one of his feuilletons, Dostoevsky has his narrator comment: "The trouble is that if anything has to be done, we become aware of it, as it were, from the outside."[6] Russians have become accustomed to uncritical acceptance of ready-made products (ideas) which are not solutions to their own historical problems because these products were shaped in totally foreign historical circumstances. By looking beyond Russia, the *intelligent*[7] has lost a vital connection with his own historical and cultural reality. He has become what for Dostoevsky was a modern horror, a "universal man" who denies the "claims of nationality,"[8] an abstraction, "an effaced coin,"[9] a citizen of the world who prides himself on an independence which, in effect, amounts to a denial of history.

A large portion of *The Diary* is devoted to the varied

current manifestations of the intelligentsia's alienation from the people. Dostoevsky repeatedly takes a specific trait of contemporary educated society and analyzes it as a consequence of "detachment from the soil." He points to the pervasiveness of lying, even about the most trivial things, among the educated class and explains it by a deeply rooted shame, a lack of self-respect which makes educated Russians feel the need to embellish the truth. Unembellished truth has come to appear alien, prosaic, unsatisfactory, and in need of adjustment. "In Russia, truth almost invariably assumes a fantastic character. In fact, men have finally succeeded in converting all that the human mind can lie about and belie into something more plausible than truth, and this prevails all over the world" (*Diary*, p. 135). But the denial of truth amounts to a basic denial of self. "This fundamental type of our society has been moulding itself over a period of two hundred years in accordance with the express principle formulated two centuries ago [i.e., by Peter the Great]: 'Never should one be himself; one should assume a different face . . . one should never resemble oneself' " (*Diary*, p. 136).

The abandonment of truth has led to a general decline in intellectual discourse, to a distortion of ideas, and to the embracing of false or debased ideas. Dostoevsky comments on the intellectual level of his time as manifested in journalism, literature, painting, argumentation by lawyers in the courtroom—in all areas of Russian educated society. And what he detects is a decline in tolerance for any idea which conflicts with those currently accepted, an impulse toward "simplication of reality," a loss of the sense of the complexity of things—what he calls "rectilinearity"—a tendency to reduce human problems to economics or psychology, a dogmatism combined with boorishness and ignorance, and a pervasive debasement of ideas ("In our midst Darwin, for example, is promptly converted into a pickpocket . . ." *Diary*, p. 604.)

Such an extreme one-sidedness and isolation, such segregation and intolerance, have developed only in our day—i.e., preeminently during the last twenty years. Coupled with these, there arose in many a man some sort of impudent boldness: men of negligible knowledge laugh—and even to one's face—at people possessing ten times more learning and understanding. And what is worst of all is that as time goes on, "rectilinearity" develops in an ever-increasing measure: for example, the instinct for adaptation, for metaphor, for allegory, begins to disappear. Noticeably, people cease (generally speaking) to understand jest, humor—and this, according to the observation of a certain German thinker, is one of the surest symptoms of the intellectual and moral degradation of an epoch. [*Diary*, p. 536]

Dostoevsky goes on to assure his reader that he is not referring only to "young ones and liberals" but also to "old ones and conservatives."

With the decline of complex thought, the sense of community, of continuity with others, of tradition dissolves and is replaced by egoism, individualism, and fragmentation. The post-reform period is marked by the repudiation of relationships, the denial of any connection with others, the refusal to recognize anything prior to oneself. Everyone begins with himself. Everyone wants to start from scratch without having to acknowledge predecessors or contemporaries. People are driven by the impulse toward immediate judgments and immediate solutions. They want, as Dostoevsky says, to take the ninth step without having taken the first eight steps. As people become more "segregated," thought becomes increasingly mechanical. People lose the ability to mediate, to see themselves and what lies beyond themselves in the proper relationship. The objects of thought are divorced from the living subject. Society, Dostoevsky implies, exists most vitally not in institutions but in people's minds, and the decline of the idea of community portends the disintegration of society itself.

Another symptom of the intelligentsia's alienation, to which Dostoevsky returns continually in *The Diary*, is its contempt for the peasantry. The civilized Russian cannot help regarding the peasantry as a mute, inert, ignorant, bestial mass. Even the educated Russians' protestations of concern for the people and their programs for improving the people's lot reveal a fundamental contempt. The *intelligent* is concerned with exteriors, with surfaces—Dostoevsky attacks his Europeanism as a veneer—and perhaps for that reason he cannot see beneath the peasant's unsavory exterior to the "solid core" of his being (*Diary*, p. 293). The educated Russian, in Dostoevsky's view, seeks to ally himself with some higher principle (Europe, science, culture, liberal and revolutionary ideas) in order to distinguish himself from the crass, benighted majority of his countrymen and prove his superiority—he is concerned above all to deny any relation to the offensive peasantry. But Dostoevsky calls him to account and charges him with responsibility for the condition of the peasantry, and in so doing refers to the legacy of serfdom: "Do not, then, reproach them [the people] for 'bestiality and ignorance,' Messrs. Wiseacres, since you—precisely you—have done nothing for them. On the contrary, you abandoned the people two centuries ago, you have forsaken them and alienated them from you; you have converted them into a taxation unit, into a quit-rent [*obrok*] item for your own benefit" (*Diary*, p. 695).

The educated Russian's excessive and deluded claims for himself, his "self-conceit" (*Diary*, p. 384), his exaggerated cosmopolitanism and abstractness are, in the final analysis, merely consequences of his lack of a foundation, of a concrete area in which to realize himself through practical activity. The serf system deprived the educated Russian of a direct relation to the land and left him with an "anguish for work." "This perpetual quest for an occupation—which is exclusively caused by our two-hundred-year long indolence and which has gone so far that at present we do not even know how to approach a task—moreover, even to determine where the task is and what it consists of—greatly irritates men in Russia" (*Diary*, p. 384). The educated Russian "was never able to gauge himself, to ascertain his forces and his significance, to determine, so to speak, his specific gravity and his real value in practical matters, in work" (*Diary*, p. 384).

In *The Diary* Dostoevsky summarizes what Russia has
acquired in her two centuries of Europeanism as "a chaos of
fragments, of sentiments, of alien, unintelligible ideas, infer-
ences, habits, but particularly words, words, words . . . nothing
but words" (*Diary*, p. 886). The Russian *intelligent* has abandoned his own language and replaced it with a jumble of
foreign words. (Dostoevsky deplores the practice prevalent
among the gentry in the eighteenth and early nineteenth centuries of raising children to speak French.) The loss of the
living Russian language is the inevitable consequence of the
educated class's detachment from the people. Indeed, Dostoevsky comments that the words "language" (*iazyk*) and "people" (*narod*) are synonyms in Russian. And he states that the
intelligent will not regain a living language until he completely merges with the people. Until such a time, "lacking
the means for structuring within himself the whole depth of
his thought and his spiritual aspirations, all his life possessing
a dead, sickly, stolen language, with timid, mechanically
learned, coarse forms which will not accommodate his
needs—he will eternally agonize as a result of an unceasing
effort and strain, both mental and moral, in the endeavor to
express his soul" (*Diary*, p. 402).

The most extreme manifestation of the educated class's
alienation is the increase in suicides among the intelligentsia,
which Dostoevsky attributes to the "loss of the sublime
meaning of life" (*Diary*, p. 542). Suicide is merely the logical
and necessary consequence of the educated Russian's separation from the people and the soil, from traditional Russian
values (Orthodoxy with its ideal of *sobornost'*, or community), and the adoption of European ideas—materialism,
atheism, socialism—which, according to Dostoevsky, lead ul-
timately to the loss of a transcendent idea capable of binding
people together. Dostoevsky asserts that a sense of the meaning of life is inseparable from a belief in God and in man's
immortality. Without the belief in his immortality, man's life
is reduced to meaningless physiological functions and be-

comes intolerable. His attempts to substitute the idea of harmony on earth for a lost immortality will fail, and his love of mankind will be poisoned by the thought of the senselessness of all human action in the face of death. Dostoevsky explains the increase in suicides in the post-emancipation period, especially among young people, by "their ugly separation from everything essential and real" (*Diary*, p. 544) and by the failure of their fathers to pass on anything for them to believe in.

Petersburg itself, the city built on the Finnish swamps at Peter the Great's command, supplies Dostoevsky with the dominant symbol of Russia's two-hundred-year alienation from herself. Petersburg is the testament in granite to one man's will to europeanize Russia. Built in a cold, damp, inhospitable environment, it lacks both a solid foundation and a connection with its surroundings. It is unreal and unnatural, and the word Dostoevsky associates with it most often, almost invariably, is "fantastic."[10] In *Winter Notes on Summer Impressions* he refers to Petersburg as "the most fantastic city with the most fantastic history of any city on the globe" (V, 57).[11] Petersburg's inhabitants are also fantastic creatures who live crowded together but in extreme isolation from one another and in the shadow of a huge, forbidding bureaucracy— creatures who are detached from reality and can fulfill themselves only in fantasy. The eclecticism and imitativeness of Petersburg's architecture testify to the city's lack of an organic identity, to the fragmentation and alienation which it imposes on its inhabitants:

In this sense, there is no city like Petersburg; from an architectural standpoint it is a reflection of all architectures in the world, of all periods and fashions: everything has been gradually borrowed and distorted in its own way. In these buildings one may read, as from a book, the tides of all ideas, and petty ideas, which, gradually or suddenly have flown to us from Europe and which have finally subdued and enslaved us. [*Diary*, p. 120]

Indeed, what is "characteristic" and "original" about Petersburg is that it "expresses its whole lack of character and its impersonality throughout the entire period of its existence" (*Diary*, p. 120). At one point in his meditation on the city, Dostoevsky extends the image of Petersburg as a structure lacking a foundation to Russia as a whole: "In these angry moments at times I would be picturing Russia as a marsh or a swamp on which someone started building a palace. On the surface, the ground appears solid and even, whereas it is something akin to the surface of pea soup: just step upon it and you will slip down into the very abyss" (*Diary*, p. 17).

The alienation which Dostoevsky describes so powerfully stems from the subversion of Russia's identity by contact with Europe. In order to overcome Russia's alienation, Dostoevsky takes pains to demonstrate that Russia's history "cannot resemble the history of other European nations" (*Diary*, p. 1033). The attempt to explain Europe's role in Russia's historical evolution and Russia's ultimate autonomy accounts for the large portion of *The Diary* in which Dostoevsky analyzes events in Europe and speaks of Europe's hold on the Russian mind. According to Dostoevsky, Russia in the post-emancipation period finds herself and Europe at the parting of the ways. She has learned all that she can learn from Europe and it is time for her to draw on her own neglected resources and to work out her own historical course. The fact that Russians have freed the serfs with land and not turned them into landless proletarians is, for Dostoevsky, proof of Russia's superiority to Europe. Furthermore, Europe, too, has evolved during the Petersburg period, and the Europe of the industrial revolution, Louis-Philippe, and 1848 was no longer the Europe of the Enlightenment which had so inspired Russia.

In Dostoevsky's view, the history of Europe can be reduced essentially to a series of displacements of one ruling group by another, each claiming universality yet each fatally determined by the struggle for political dominance. The struggle for power is accompanied by increasing social fragmentation. The hallmark of modern Europe for Dostoevsky is "segregation" (*obosoblenie*) of society into smaller and smaller units, each contending against the others and each considering itself the sole possessor of truth. Any general idea, or sense of community, which could counteract or diminish this fragmentation has been lost. Europe is affected by segregation at every level of its social life, as manifested in its national rivalries, class struggles, and extreme individualism.

Dostoevsky traces Europe's contemporary conflict to the origins of European society. He locates the European essence in what he calls "the Roman idea," the belief that the political organization of society must precede the achievement of brotherhood and justice. According to Dostoevsky, this idea has dominated Europe throughout its two-thousand-year history and underlies all political forms that Europe has produced: the Roman Empire, the Catholic Church, the French Republic, socialism, and even Protestantism. All European political forms are descendants of the Roman Empire with its doctrine of conquest and temporal power. Western Christianity—Catholicism—took over the Roman project of founding a universal empire and thereby made a distinction between the Church's activity in the world (in the here-and-now) and its transhistorical mission in the name of Christ. It split off its activity of attaining power in the world from God and relegated Him to the hereafter. The Pope then usurped the place of God in the world from which He had been banished. Europe has thus forsaken Christ, i.e., the idea of the unity and brotherhood of all men and the idea of individual freedom, for material and political power. Europe's history is one of continuous conflict because there is no higher authority that could arbitrate in earthly disputes, and because (temporary) security can be achieved only at the expense of another group, by suppressing an enemy. Once the primary principle of the unity of all men has been abandoned (or relegated to the future), society becomes increasingly splintered, and attempts to achieve a common rational goal lead necessarily to coercion and further division.

In Europe, the name of Christ has become merely another instrument in the struggle for power. The only difference between the Catholics and other political forces is that the Catholics mask their purely political motives with hypocritical appeals to Christ and the Gospels. (For this reason, perhaps, Dostoevsky regards the Catholics as the most dangerous destabilizing party in Europe and attributes tremendous importance to their machinations.) Socialism, which openly proposes to unite humanity by appealing to universal human nature instead of to Christ, is pursuing the same goal as Catholicism but without the latter's deception. Both Catholicism and socialism, as far as Dostoevsky is concerned, are predicated on the rejection of Christ, on atheism, and on the organization of society for narrow political purposes. Dostoevsky argues that socialism is a direct descendant of Catholicism—in other words, that socialism, which appears to be a new, revolutionary doctrine, is merely another in a series of repetitions of the quintessential European idea:

The present-day French socialism itself—seemingly an ardent and fatal protest against the Catholic idea on the part of all men and nations tortured and strangulated with it, who desire by all means to live, and without its gods—this protest itself, which actually began at the end of the last century, is nothing but the truest and most direct continuation of the Catholic idea, its fullest, most final realization, its fatal consequence which has been evolved through the centuries. French socialism is nothing else but a compulsory communion of mankind—an idea which dates back to ancient Rome, and which was fully conserved in Catholicism. Thus the idea of the liberation of the human spirit from Catholicism became vested there precisely in the narrowest Catholic forms borrowed from the very heart of its spirit, from its letter, from its materialism, from its despotism, from its morality. [Diary, p. 563]

From his vantage point, Dostoevsky perceives what he takes to be the insidious continuity and repetition which overtakes and makes a mockery of all attempts to change European society. The logic of displacement ensures that a new usurper of power will only reproduce the situation he set out to change. He, in turn, will have to consolidate his power against other groups and to exclude from power those in whose name he claims to rule. (This inescapable logic which ensures the betrayal of all ideals once they enter the political arena reminds one of Shigalev's paradox in *The Possessed*— "Starting out with absolute freedom, I arrive at absolute despotism"—and of the Grand Inquisitor's dilemma, as well as of the aborted attempts of other characters in Dostoevsky's novels to change society. These betrayals, or ironic reversals, underscore the weight of history, which tricks those who think they can make a clean break with it.) Dostoevsky emphasizes the continuity and essential unity of European political forms in order to demonstrate that Europe has exhausted all the possibilities open to it and has nothing to offer Russia.

France, which Dostoevsky concentrates on as the key actor in Europe's political conflicts, provides a paradigm of the logic of displacement, exclusion, and segregation. Dostoevsky dwells on the Third Republic as the most extreme instance of the disintegration of stable political forms, as the latest stage in the evolution of the Roman idea in a Europe on the verge of total disintegration. Like Marx in his dissection of the short-lived Second Republic (in "The Eighteenth Brumaire of Louis Bonaparte"), Dostoevsky, with almost equal disdain, comments on the incongruity of the republic, its inherent instability and duplicity. The republic which appeals to the old revolutionary slogan of "Liberty, Equality, Fraternity" and claims to uphold the rights of all men is in fact more hostile to the working class than was the old regime. And it is the locus of new and more complex segregations than those of the old regime. The republic has more near neighbors than the old regime, which was at the apex of the social pyramid, and these rivals will become its most fierce enemies: "There is a political—perhaps even natural— law which says that two powerful and adjacent neighbors, no matter how friendly, always in the long run seek to annihilate each other and sooner or later they do succeed in their scheme" (*Diary*, p. 253). Not only does the bourgeoisie find itself threatened by both the remnants of the old regime and by the "demos," but it is divided against itself. The majority of the bourgeoisie detests the republic and longs for a dictatorship to protect its interests.

By its triumph in 1789 and its subsequent ascendancy, the bourgeoisie laid the conditions for its future confrontation with "the humiliated and the defrauded," "all those who had not received their share in the new formula of universal unity proclaimed by the French Revolution of 1789" (*Diary*, p. 729). Dostoevsky, like Marx, sees the bourgeoisie creating the conditions for its own demise. The bourgeoisie inherited the wealth of the old regime (in the form of the estates of the emigrants and the Church, which it split up and sold), and even if this wealth was divided among more people than formerly, it gave the bourgeoisie something to defend at all costs against the demos (*Diary*, p. 252). The bourgeoisie, having replaced the nobility, put a stop to the course of democratization and chose the republic as the best means for maintaining its interests (*Diary*, p. 254). Now the republic is threatened by the excluded demos who, according to Dostoevsky, are motivated by envy and resentment, by the desire to occupy the place of the bourgeoisie—in other words, a reactive, negative motivation—and by Catholicism (which is trying to ally itself with the demos).

But the most dreadful thing in this connection is the fact that aside from everything fantastic, there developed a most cruel and inhuman tendency which is by no means fantastic, but indeed, quite real and historically inevitable. It is fully expressed in the saying: "Ote-toi de là, que je m'y mette!" . . . To millions of the demos—save for all too rare exceptions—the plunder of property-owners is the principal object, the crown of all desires. Yet one cannot blame the paupers: the oligarchs themselves have kept them in ignorance to such an extent that, save for insignificant exceptions, all these millions of wretched and blind people, no doubt, actually and most naïvely believe that they will enrich themselves precisely as a result of this robbery, and that the whole social idea, which their ringleaders preach to them, consists exactly of this. Besides, how can they understand their ringleader-dreamers or any of their prophecies about science? Nevertheless, they will unquestionably be victorious and, if the rich do not yield in good time, dreadful things will ensue. But nobody is going to yield in good time—maybe, because the time for concessions is over. Nor will the paupers themselves desire them; they would reject any accord even if they were given everything; they would keep thinking that they were being misled and cheated. They wish to take the law into their own hands. [*Diary*, pp. 252-53]

The segregation of the parties has assumed such proportions that the state organism has been utterly demolished, beyond the possibility of repair . . . . It is this phantom of wholeness that the unhappy bourgeois—and with them a multitude of naïve people in Europe—continue to treat as a living force of the organism, deceiving themselves with hope and at the same time trembling from fear and hatred. Oligarchs are thinking only about the interests of the rich; democracy is thinking only about the interests of the poor—but commonweal, the good of all people and the future of France as a whole—is at present nobody's concern there, save of socialistic and positivistic dreamers . . . . [*Diary*, pp. 251-52]

Whether the current upheaval results in communism or a Catholic tyranny, Dostoevsky believes the liquidation of the republic in France will in all probability lead to a second round of war with Germany in which Germany will attempt to crush France totally, not half-heartedly as in 1871. Writing in 1877, Dostoevsky expects and even looks forward to a general conflagration which will consume the political orders of Old Europe. He sees no possibility of avoiding a final clash between Catholic France and Protestant Germany which will inevitably draw in the other powers of Europe. Russia will be the decisive factor in this final convulsion and will, if necessary, Dostoevsky says, help Germany liquidate Catholicism.

Catholicism has been chosen as the common banner for rallying the whole old order of things—the product of nineteen centuries. This is an alliance against something new and forthcoming, essential and fateful, against the impending renovation of the universe through a new order of things; against the social, moral and fundamental revolution in the whole of Western European life . . . . against the dreadful concussion and the colossal revolution which undeniably threatens to shake all the bourgeois states throughout the world, wherever the bourgeoisie has organized and flourished after the French pattern of 1789, and to overthrow it and take its place. [*Diary*, p. 721]

The point is that, to my way of thinking, the present period, too, will end in Old Europe with something colossal, i.e., perhaps not literally identical with the events which brought an end to the eighteenth century, but nevertheless, equally gigantic, elemental, and dreadful—also entailing a change of the face of the whole world, or at least, in the west of Old Europe. [*Diary*, p. 724]

The approaching war will signal the rebirth of Europe, so that one should not seek to postpone it:

Oh, no doubt, this would be a dreadful affair should so much human blood be shed! But at least there is a consolation . . . . so many new and progressive things would ensue in human relationships that perhaps it is not necessary to suffer spiritually and to dread too much the last convulsive jerk of Old Europe on the eve of her indubitable and great regeneration. [*Diary*, p. 834]

Against the background of Europe's social and national conflicts, Russia, in spite of her 150-year schism between the intelligentsia and the people, offers the hope of a new solution to the problem on which Europe is foundering—the problem of social differentiation and the suppression of the proletariat by the bourgeoisie. "There can be no question of any class struggle in our country; on the contrary, the classes in our country tend to merge."[12] In spite of the breach caused by Peter the Great, each of the two classes still sees itself as Russian. By freeing the serfs "with land"[13] Alexander II avoided the European course of turning the peasantry into a proletariat.

There in the West they consider the extreme and most unattainable ideal of prosperity something that we have already possessed for a long time . . . every human being, on emerging from his mother's womb, is already registered as belonging to a piece of land, so that he really should not die of hunger.[14]

Why did liberation proceed in Europe not from the owners, barons and country squires, but from uprisings and rebellions, from fire and sword and rivers of blood? And if, here and there, liberation was accomplished without rivers of blood, everywhere, without exception, it was carried out on proletarian principles; a people was set free as perfect slaves. [Diary, p. 291]

It is by virtue of her solution to the problem of social differentiation that Russia will renew herself and offer a new historical perspective to the fragmented societies of the West. Russia alone of all European countries, because of her long-standing independent religious and cultural tradition dating back to the split between the Roman Catholic Church and the Orthodox Eastern Church, offers the prospect of avoiding Europe's disintegration and of realizing a new model for the organization of society which is essentially different from those produced by European history. Russia, too, is afflicted with this "segregation of units and the extreme, so to speak, chemical decomposition of our society into component parts, which has suddenly occurred in our time" (Diary, p. 249). But in Russia, Dostoevsky contends, segregation has taken place mainly within the educated class, which he refers to as a "bundle of twigs that has fallen apart" (we will see shortly that Dostoevsky was poignantly aware of another kind of segregation in Russia which had nothing to do with the educated class):

there is still hope that the bundle will again be rejoined [in Russia]. But over there, in Europe, no bundle will ever be tied together; there, everything has become segregated in a manner different from ours—maturely, clearly and with precision; there groups and units are living their last days, and they themselves are aware of it; they refuse to cede anything one to the other; they would rather die than yield. [Diary, p. 250]

Dostoevsky dwells on Europe and its history in order to support his conviction that Europe is essentially different from Russia. Europe is expiring just at the moment when Russia has rediscovered her unique popular traditions of the *obshchina*, the *mir*, and the *zemskii sobor*,[15] when the educated elite has shown signs of turning toward the people, and when the Tsar has, by the emancipation edict, given proof of Russia's ability to solve social problems by sacrifice rather than by class conflict. But sixteen years after the emancipation, Dostoevsky has doubts about how clearly the difference between Russia and Europe is recognized by the intelligentsia. He senses that Russia's future course depends upon such a recognition on the part of the intelligentsia and the government, since precisely those features which Russia can point to as distinguishing her social life from that of the West are in danger of succumbing to the forces of modernization and capitalism. At this critical point in Russia's history, Europe offers Russia an image of what she could easily become and what she must avoid at all costs.

If Europe represents a negative pole for Russia's identity, the people represent a positive pole—the sole remedy for Russia's illness. In spite of their poverty and backwardness, their corruption and drunkenness, the people, according to Dostoevsky, have preserved intact their faith in Christ and their sense of morality and community. The people are in possession of "unconscious ideas" which are the source of their "vigorous and animated life" (*Diary*, p. 15). These moral or religious ideas which are alive in the people are what Europe has repudiated, and they constitute for Dostoevsky the foundation of all civic ideas and all social institutions (*Diary*, p. 1000). The unconscious nature of these ideas is a guarantee of their spontaneity and power (which are embodied in such legendary and poetic figures as Ilya Muromets and Nekrasov's Vlas); they emanate from the deepest recesses of the Russian soil.

One such idea, which contrasts sharply with Europe's

"Roman idea," is the people's belief that the spiritual unity of mankind must precede any lasting political organization. Another idea through which the people manifest their moral power is their attitude toward crime and the criminal, which implies an attitude toward society as a whole. Dostoevsky speaks of the people's attitude toward crime early in *The Diary* and opposes it to Europe's two solutions to the problem of criminality, and, by extension, to the attitude toward criminality prevalent among the Russian intelligentsia. The people, Dostoevsky says, neither exclude the criminal from society (the bourgeois solution), nor do they justify crime on the basis of the "environment" (the socialist solution). Rather, they look upon the criminal as an "unfortunate," as a "sufferer" and are "aware that they themselves are guilty in common with every criminal" (*Diary*, p. 15).

The people have retained a feeling for society, not as an abstraction but as an aggregate of living, suffering, concrete individuals. They have not been "educated" to see society through the categories of institutions, laws, science or to explain and justify behavior in terms of the "environment" and "psychology." According to Dostoevsky, the people may commit evil, but they are aware of having done so and do not try to avoid assuming responsibility for their actions. They believe in the value of work, suffering, and self-sacrifice, and their actions manifest their thirst for truth (*Diary*, pp. 616, 985). Man has not been eliminated from their view of society. In this crucial sense, the people have escaped the alienation that is endemic in Europe and in the Russian intelligentsia.

Above all, the people inspire in Dostoevsky the hope that Russia, owing to her backwardness and her "organic," traditional institutions, can bypass the evils associated with capitalism and can achieve a higher order of social organization. This hope, which Andrzej Walicki has called "the privilege of backwardness,"[16] is something that Dostoevsky shares with the Russian populists, who argued that Russia could skip (or at least shorten) the capitalist phase of development and attain a cooperative, socialist society based on institutions like the peasant commune and the *artel'* (a cooperative association of workers). In the populists' view, Russia was fortunate to have been spared the growth of a large bourgeoisie and the proletarianization of the peasantry. She could thus hope to preserve those healthy, positive features of peasant agrarian organization which had been destroyed in the West and to cultivate them as the nucleus of a new cooperative, truly human society. The crucial difference between Russia and the West—the advantage associated with Russia's backwardness—raised the possibility that Russia could learn from Europe's mistakes and achieve socialism not through violent revolution but merely by preserving and fostering its already existing traditional institutions. As Nikolai Mikhailovsky put it in 1872:

The worker's question in Europe is a revolutionary question because its solution consists in giving the means of production back to the producers, that is, in the expropriation of the present proprietors. The worker's question in Russia is a *conservative* question because its solution consists merely in keeping the means of production in the hands of the producers, that is, *in protecting the present proprietors against expropriation.* [Emphasis added][17]

Dostoevsky fully shared this view: "all that they [Russian Westerners] seek in Europe has already long been existent in Russia—at least in embryo and as a potentiality—and . . . it even constitutes her substance, only not in a revolutionary guise . . ." (*Diary*, p. 354).

Throughout *The Diary* Dostoevsky expresses his faith in Russia's originality and superiority over Europe and his conviction that the people will, in the end, *express themselves*, will utter their word, will manifest their enormous moral strength to the surprise of Europe and the Russian intelligentsia.

Vlas will come to his senses and will take up God's labor. . . . He will save himself and us, since—I repeat once more—light and salvation will come from below . . . . [*Diary*, pp. 42–43]

I even believe that the reign of reason and light may be inaugurated in our Russia, perhaps even sooner than elsewhere, since even now, in Russia, no one would favor the idea of the necessity of bestializing one part of the people for the well-being of another part representing civilization as we find it all over Europe. [*Diary*, p. 189]

At least in Russia, the land and the commune—I admit they are in a most miserable state—constitute the great nucleus of the future idea . . . .[*Diary*, p. 418]

At the same time, does it [the commune] not contain the grain of something new, a better future ideal which awaits all men, . . . and which can come to pass only in Russia, since it will come not through war and rebellion, but again, by great and universal consensus? [*Diary*, p. 420]

Our destitute land will, perhaps, at length, speak a new word to the world.[*Diary*, p. 961]

Dostoevsky's hope in the people and their institutions puts him in the same difficult situation as the populists. Like them, he both wants to assert that the people can preserve their values in spite of the increasing encroachments and pressures on their traditional way of life by the forces of the market and industrialism, and he is forced to acknowledge that it is precisely the positive resources of the people and the promise of an alternative to Europe which are in danger of being destroyed in the post-emancipation period.

A large portion of *The Diary* is devoted to the symptoms of corruption and social differentiation among the peasantry: drunkenness, fragmentation, the disintegration of the commune, migration to the factory, increasing ensnarement into the money economy, reliance on money as the supreme value. At certain points in *The Diary*, after alluding to the miserable situation of the peasantry, Dostoevsky contemplates, if only to reject emphatically, the possibility that the Russian peasantry is in danger of being turned into a landless proletariat. It is at such moments, we can assume, that the image of England and the industrial revolution which exerted such power on the imaginations of Russian intellectuals (in the Russian translations of novels by Dickens and Elizabeth Gaskell, and in the engravings of Gustave Doré) rises before Dostoevsky's eyes. Dostoevsky was at one with the populists in his sense of urgency at what he saw as the threat to the peasant's way of life, to the moral values associated with that way of life and, consequently, to Russia's future. He shared with the populists the fear that if something were not done to stop the course of social differentiation and to protect the peasant institutions, Russia would be on her way to repeating the experience of Western Europe.

This fear is expressed vividly in the writings of several of the populists: especially Tkachev, Flerovsky, and Mikhailovsky. Tkachev, for example, saw the major task of what he called the "party of progress" as stopping the "chaotic process of differentiation which has been caused by retrogressive historical movement . . . ."[18] He felt the urgent need for intervention in the process of capitalist development and social differentiation:

Already the commune is beginning to collapse; the government is doing everything possible to destroy it once and for all. Among the peasants a class of kulaks is growing up, who buy and hire out the land of the peasants and nobles, a sort of peasant aristocracy. The free movement of landed property from owner to owner becomes less difficult every day; the widening of agrarian credit, and the development of monetary transactions, increase each day. The gentry are compelled, willy-nilly, to make improvements in their agricultural systems. Such progress is usually accompanied by a development of national industry and an increase in town life. And so in Russia at this time all the conditions are there for the formation on one side of a very strong conservative class of peasants, landowners and farmers; and on the other side a bourgeoisie of money, trade, industry—capitalists in fact. As these classes come into being and grow stronger, the situation of the people will inevitably grow worse, and the chances for the success of a violent revolution will grow more and more problematical. That is why we cannot wait.[19]

For Tkachev, perhaps more intensely than for any other of the populists, Russian history stood at a critical juncture

where for a short time, two different paths for future development were possible: one leading to the pauperization of the
masses and the class struggles associated with capitalist society in the West; the other leading to what Tkachev called
"organic physiological equality" introduced by the dictatorship of a revolutionary vanguard in order to "har-
monize . . . the needs of all individuals in accordance with the
means of satisfying those needs."[20] The extreme nature of
Tkachev's program for avoiding capitalist development (a
program which has been compared to Leninism, but which is
even closer to Maoism) is a measure of the urgency with
which certain observers, including Dostoevsky, viewed Russia's predicament in the post-emancipation period. The tone
of urgency in Tkachev's writings runs through *The Diary*, and
the problem of the will to instantaneous, total transformation
of society, exemplified by Tkachev's program, is one that
Dostoevsky probes throughout his later fiction.

The recurrent themes of *The Diary* all point up the uncertainty of the historical moment in Russia—the precarious
position of the peasantry; the lack of a common moral foundation or shared values, tendencies toward "segregation," isolation, and laws that promote individual and group conflicts;
pride in autonomy; and pride in power over others, which
becomes a goal in itself.

The importance assumed by money, especially after the
liberation of the serfs, is one of Dostoevsky's central motifs
for the drive toward power, isolation, and distinction which
spreads and infects more and more people, making them
more and more homogeneous. Money represents a new kind
of abstract relation which is primarily a denial of relation, an
assertion of absolute autonomy.

almost the whole present-day world is conceiving freedom in terms
of financial security and laws guaranteeing it: "I have money, and
therefore I can do what I please; I have money, and therefore I am
not going to perish and I will not ask for anyone's help, and to not
have to ask for anyone's help is the highest freedom." And yet, in

reality, this is not freedom but, again, slavery, slavery based on money. On the contrary, the highest freedom is not to hoard money and not to base one's security upon it, but to "distribute one's property among all people and to serve everybody." [*Diary*, p. 623]

By materialism, in this case, I mean the worship of money by the people, their adoration of the power inherent in the bag of gold.[*Diary*, p. 187]

I repeat: something permeated with materialism and scepticism is soaring in the air: an adoration of gratuitous gain, of enjoyment without labor . . . . [*Diary*, pp. 188–89]

It stands to reason that this former rich merchant worshiped his million as God: in his view the million was everything; the million had extricated him out of nothingness and had made him impressive. . . . "With money I can buy everything, every distinction, every valor; I can bribe anybody and I can bail myself out of anything."[*Diary*, pp. 485–86]

Now the former limits of the merchant of earlier days were *suddenly, in our day*, widely set asunder. Suddenly he became affiliated with the European speculator, *hitherto unknown in Russia* and the stock-exchange gambler . . . . Nowadays he himself is somebody . . . all of a sudden he found himself decidedly in one of the highest places in society. [*Diary*, p. 486; emphasis added]

Briefly, he becomes more and more wholeheartedly convinced that it is precisely he who nowadays is "the best" man on earth, in lieu of all the former ones. But the impending calamity is not that he entertains such nonsense, but the fact that others also, it would seem (and already quite a few), begin to reason in the same way. In our day, the money-bag is unquestionably conceived by a dreadful majority to be the best of everything. Of course these fears will be disputed. However, our present-day factual veneration of the money-bag is not only indisputable, but by reason of the proportions it has assumed, it is also unprecedented. I repeat: in the past too the power of the money-bag was understood in Russia by everybody, *but never until now has the money-bag been regarded as the loftiest thing on earth.* In the official classification of Russians—in the social hierarchy—the former merchant's money-bag could not outweigh even a bureaucrat. *At present, however,* even the former hierarchy, without any coercion from the outside, seems to be ready to remove itself to second place, ceding its place to the lovely and beautiful "condition" of the best man "who for so long a time and so erroneously did not assume his true rights." [Diary, pp. 486-87; emphasis added]

The old has either been destroyed or is worn out; the new is still borne on the wings of fantasy, whereas in actual life we behold something abominable which has reached unheard of proportions. The fascination which is attributed to this new force—the money-bag—even begins to inspire fear in some hearts, which are all too suspicious, for instance, as regards the people. Indeed, even though we—the upper stratum of society—might be seduced by the new idol, nevertheless we should not vanish without a trace; not in vain has the torch of education been shining for us throughout two centuries. We are armed with enlightenment, and we should be able to repel the monster. . . . But our people—that "inert, corrupt, insensible mass"—into which the Jew has thrust himself, what are they going to set against the monster of materialism, in the guise of the money-bag, marching on them? Their misery? Their rags? Their taxes and their bad harvests? Their vices? Liquor? Flogging? We were afraid that the people would forthwith fall prostrate before the increasing power of the money-bag, and that before even one generation should pass they would be driven into submission not only through coercion, but that they would submit morally, with their whole will. [Diary, p. 488]

The emergence of money as the ultimate value has undermined the values associated with the old aristocracy. It has displaced all the old social bonds and human relations. An external, abstract, impersonal substance has taken on universal power. Since money is an abstraction from individual qualities, it frees the individual from all bonds. It is a hardened, congealed form of power which people aspire to in order to protect themselves in a society which has lost its traditional ties.

In the passages quoted above, Dostoevsky conveys the same sense of a disruption and inversion of social relations and values as Marx when the latter speaks, in the "Economic and Philosophic Manuscripts," of money as the "confusion and transposition of all things . . . of all natural and human qualities."[21] Dostoevsky suggests that a terrible change has taken place in Russian society since the emancipation of the serfs, and that money is the symptom of this change. Pursuing another of Marx's ideas, we can conjecture that what happened with the advent of money—not simply as a medium of exchange, but as capital, as a form of power over others—is that the economy, which in feudal times was subordinate to the political-social order,[22] became an autonomous realm and even the dominant force in society. It took on a life of its own independent of politics, morality, and religion and began to exert its influence in all spheres of life. The change appears to both Marx and Dostoevsky as a break with a more human and more natural society of the past.

The desire for money and the juggernaut of economic freedom threaten to destroy the commune, which for Dostoevsky as for the Slavophiles and the populists justifies Russia's claim to a path of historical development different from Western Europe's. In the commune Russia has kept intact the kernel of an egalitarian society based on the periodic redistribution of land and the sharing of social burdens. Now, with the emancipation, increasing differentiation among the peasantry, and the increasing accumulation of land by rich peasants and merchants, the freed peasant is in danger of losing his land and of entering on economic servitude which will replace personal bondage to his former master.

Our people, liberated by the great word of the Monarch, are inexperienced . . . and they are merely taking the first strides along the new road: this is an enormous and extraordinary break; it is almost wholly unexpected, almost unheard of in history by reason of its completeness and character. These first and now independent steps of the liberated giant along the new path, fraught with great peril, require extraordinary caution. And yet, what did our people encounter at these first steps?—Vacillation among the upper strata of society; the alienation from the people of our intelligentsia which, for centuries, has been in existence (this is the principal thing), and on top of these—trash and the Jew. [Diary, p. 104]

Almost half of our present budget is paid for by vodka; in other words, this means that, judging by the present, the whole future of the people is dependent upon national drunkenness and popular depravity. We are paying, so to speak, with our future for our stately budget of a great European power. We are cutting the tree at the very root, in order to get at the fruit as quickly as possible. [*Diary*, p. 104]

Genuine, sound capital accumulates in a country in no other way than by being based on a general labor prosperity; otherwise only capital owned by kulaks and Jews can come into existence . . . . If the people should fail to come to their senses, they, as a whole, will find themselves in a very short time in the hands of all sorts of Jews, and in such an event no commune is going to save them: there will be merely uniformly equal paupers, mortgaged and enslaved as a whole commune, while in their stead, Jews and kulaks will be providing the money for the budget. There will emerge petty, depraved and mean little *bourgeois* and a countless number of paupers enslaved by them—such will be the picture! Yiddishers will be soaking up the blood of the people and subsisting on their debauch and humiliation; inasmuch, however, as they—these Yiddishers—will provide money for the budget, they will be supported. This is only a bad, horrible dream and . . . it is merely a fancy!—titular councilor Poprishchin's dream I concede. But it will not come true! More than once before have the people saved themselves. [*Diary*, pp. 105-6]

After giving free rein to his worst fears, Dostoevsky habitually dismisses them with the summary assertion that the people will save themselves, will manifest their enormous hidden strength and that Russia will not go the way of Europe. But his disclaimers appear weak and unconvincing beside the intensity and vividness of his fears. It is not surprising that the symptoms of Russia's historical confusion which Dostoevsky dwells on in *The Diary* are also the central themes of his later fiction, written in the twenty years following the emancipation. And in the fiction, the fears about segregation, social differentiation, and the loss of values dominate the authorial consciousness and are not easily dismissed.

We have seen that Russia, according to Dostoevsky, stands at a critical juncture in her historical development.

The post-reform period is one of deep confusion and conflict
in Russian society. A chasm separates the intelligentsia from
the people. The intelligentsia still finds itself under the influence of European ideas and forms which, as Dostoevsky attempts to demonstrate, have doomed Europe to destruction.
At the same time, the progress of capitalism in Russia itself
threatens to destroy the traditional life of the people—the
repository of Russia's living values, Russia's hope for an organic, communal society as opposed to the individualistic
"antheap" societies of Western Europe.

It is as responses to this awareness of being at a critical
juncture that we must examine Dostoevsky's ideas on literature and his nationalism. Both represent attempts to salvage
something positive and distinctive in Russia's fragmented
past, something which provides a promise of a future identity.
Both are means of mediating between the people and the
intelligentsia, and between an eccentric present and a harmonious future.

The most urgent task facing Russia, in Dostoevsky's
view, in the post-emancipation period is the reconciliation of
the intelligentsia with the people—the *merging* which was the
aim of so many Russian thinkers in the 1870s and which led
to the dramatic though ill-fated "To the People" movement.[23]

Writing in 1861, Dostoevsky says that the *intelligent* has
become conscious that "it is impossible for us to go any further by ourselves alone; we require all the forces of the Russian spirit to help our further development."[24] He cautions,
however, against underestimating the breadth of the chasm
that separates the two classes of Russian society. In the first
of two articles entitled "Pedantry and Literacy" published in
Vremja (July 1861) he argues that educated Russians, even
those who consider themselves experts on the life of the common people, do not really know the people because "they
have never lived with the people but have lived another, separate, special kind of life."[25] If ignorance of the people on the

part of the educated Russian constitutes one obstacle to merging with the people, the intelligentsia's culture represents another.

Dostoevsky maintains, however, that the intelligentsia, in spite of its alienation, has acquired something positive from its European experience, and something that the people need—namely, its culture and exposure to other nations. The intelligentsia, for all its loss of substance, still has something of value to contribute to Russia's future identity, and this contribution lies, for Dostoevsky, in literacy and literature.

Dostoevsky reveals his ambivalent and complex feelings about the intelligentsia's European experience and its problematic relation to the people in a remarkable passage in *The Diary*:

It is we who have to bow before the people and await from them everything—both thought and expression; it is we who must bow before the people's truth and recognize it as such . . . . In a word, we must bow like prodigal children who, for two hundred years, have been absent from home, but who nevertheless have returned Russians—which, by the way, is our great merit. On the other hand, however, we must bow on one condition only, and this—*sine qua non*: that the people accept from us those numerous things which we have brought with us. Indeed, we cannot completely exterminate ourselves in the face of the people, or even—before any truth of theirs, whatever it may be. Let us keep what is our own, and for nothing in the world shall we part with it, not even—if it should come to this—for the happiness of union with the people. Otherwise, let us separate and let us both perish apart. But there will never be an "otherwise." And I am firmly convinced that this *something* which we have brought with us really does exist, it is not a mirage but possesses both form and weight. Nevertheless, I repeat, there is much ahead of us that is an enigma—so much, in fact that one dreads to keep on waiting. [*Diary*, pp. 204-5]

This passage conveys by its syntax, its oscillations between apparent contraries, its vagueness of reference combined with aggressivity of assertion, its negative affirmations, and, finally, its vague admission of apprehension about the future the depth of the conflicting claims exerted on Dostoevsky by the ideas of the "people" and the intelligentsia and by the problem of reconciling them. One might ask what it means to "bow before the people" and their truth and to "await from them everything—both thought and expression" if the intelligentsia must not relinquish its own truth. Presumably the two truths can somehow be harmonized, and the prodigal son must not renounce the valuable experience he has acquired during his wanderings. Still, the people's truth is as yet an unknown quantity which awaits both thought and expression, and the references to what the intelligentsia has accomplished and to what it is bringing home are equally vague ("those numerous things which we have brought with us"; "this *something* which we have brought with us really does exist; it is not a mirage but possesses both form and weight"). Dostoevsky seems compelled to champion both sides of the misunderstanding. Along with the desire to bow before the people goes a fear of engulfment, of annihilation ("completely exterminate ourselves in the face of the people"). The alternatives are extreme: either salvation and harmony (which remain unmentioned and problematic here, though implied) or destruction ("let us both perish apart"). Stylistically, if one can talk of style here, this passage reflects in a poignant way Dostoevsky's uncertainty about the relation between the two classes of Russian society and, at the same time, his determination that a reconciliation be effected between them.

The two articles entitled "Pedantry and Literacy," written in 1861, contain an extended discussion of the means of reconciling the two classes of Russian society. Here Dostoevsky asserts that the only way to bridge the gulf between the intelligentsia and the people is by fostering the growth of education and, specifically, of literacy. The implication in the light of the later passage from *The Diary* (written fifteen years later, in 1876) quoted above is that only when the peasants achieve literacy and an appreciation of books and ideas will they be able to accept the treasure which the intelligentsia brings to them from its European phase.

Literacy and literature—the lowest and highest rungs on the ladder of culture, it would appear, for Dostoevsky—are seen by him as the two means by which the intelligentsia and the people can come to know each other and thus reach a reconciliation. Dostoevsky begins the discussion of the problem of fostering literacy among the people by saying that "all that has been written by us, the whole of our modern and old literature, is no good as reading matter for the common people."[26] Starting with this sobering appraisal of the situation, Dostoevsky goes on to say that it is for the educated class to take the first step "because they were the first to shy away from the people."[27] The correct solution to the problem of literacy depends upon the ability of the intelligentsia (and especially of those who see themselves as enlighteners of the people) to adopt an attitude of respect for the individuality of the people. The question is not one of the mechanics of teaching illiterate peasants to read but rather one of "arousing in the common people a desire for reading."[28] By concocting special "readers" for the peasants, philanthropic enlighteners will only increase the peasants' awareness of the gap between themselves and their masters, since the artificial and condescending tone of the primers will not escape the peasants' notice. What is called for, Dostoevsky argues, is a basic change in orientation on the part of the intelligentsia: "There is something that we, their masters, who are trying to teach them are ignorant of, so that we have first of all to learn something from them, and that is why they really have no respect for all our learning . . . . And the common people could teach us a lot, if only, for example, how we are to teach them."[29] Thus, even the first step in this long process of reconciliation requires the establishment of a more reciprocal relation between the two parties. One of the few concrete acts of reform that Dostoevsky advocates in his journalism, and the one he considers most imperative, is the teaching of reading to the peasantry. Throughout his writings, the image of an alienated member of the upper class teaching a peasant to read offers an example of the concrete, practical activity which, according to Dostoevsky, is desperately needed in post-emancipation Russia.

Literacy seems to have a dual function for Dostoevsky in the reunification of Russian society. It will enable the people to give expression to *their* truth, and it will enable them to understand and to evaluate the experience of the intelligentsia since the Petrine reforms.

The importance of literature, which of course is the product of the upper class alone, as Dostoevsky stresses, consists of the fact that it "is today one of the main manifestations of Russian conscious life. We received everything from outside and gratis, beginning with science and ending with the most ordinary things in life, but literature we obtained by our own efforts, it is a product of our own life."[30] Literature draws on the sources of national life—on language and popular culture—and articulates the problems and aspirations of a people at a given moment in their history. Literature is not a reflection of a prosaic, statistical, external reality, but grasps what is essential—the underlying structure of reality. Although it is an autonomous realm, literature still has its roots in history and exerts its own influence on history. By giving intelligible form to historical problems, it can articulate new historical needs and can lead to the creation of new facts. Literature stakes out a privileged area in which a nation becomes conscious of itself, or rather in which it constitutes its identity.

Pushkin embodies for Dostoevsky the positive legacy of the Russian intelligentsia and the Petersburg period, the "treasure" that the intelligentsia has to offer the people—the single redeeming aspect of the intelligentsia's long period of detachment from the people. According to Dostoevsky, Pushkin introduced into Russian literature an awareness of Russia's unique historical identity. Although Pushkin came from the gentry and although he had absorbed European culture, he nevertheless represents the supreme embodiment of the

Russian national spirit, that is, the spirit of the people. Pushkin accomplished in literature one hundred years after Peter
the Great what Peter attempted to accomplish on a historical
plane. He not only assimilated the languages and the literary
and national traditions of Europe but was able to use these
means to give unprecedented expression to dilemmas that
were peculiarly Russian. Pushkin, no matter how much he
was steeped in European culture, always created new and
original forms which sprang from his awareness of his own
cultural identity as a Russian. Peter suffers from the comparison with Pushkin. Dostoevsky says that although Peter's work
contains "a great deal of truth," the "form of his activity
was . . . perhaps mistaken. The fact of the transformation was
correct but its forms were not Russian, not national, and
quite often were in direct and fundamental contradiction of
the Russian national spirit."[31]

Amid the alienation and superficial Europeanism of the
Petersburg period, Pushkin offers the promise of a strong
identity. Hence his tremendous importance for Dostoevsky.
Dostoevsky says of Pushkin that he "was the first to detect
and record the principal pathological phenomenon of our
educated society historically detached from the people" (Diary, p. 959). Furthermore, he says, Pushkin was "the first to
comfort us by giving us the great hope that this is not a
mortal illness, that Russian society can be cured, reformed
and resurrected, if it embraces the people's truth" (Diary, p.
960). Thus, Pushkin was the first to illuminate the darkness
and alienation of the Petersburg period. Dostoevsky calls him
a "guiding light," a "promise for the future," "a prophecy,"
and "a revelation" (Diary, p. 967). In him, Dostoevsky sees
exemplified Russia's two crucial national traits: her reliance
on the common people and "her universal susceptibility and
responsiveness, her profound kinship with the geniuses of all
ages and nations of the world" (Diary, p. 784). Pushkin's
strong identity allowed him to reincarnate himself in alien
peoples. According to Dostoevsky, Pushkin actually became

what he described: "He was a man of the ancient world; he was a German; he was an Englishman . . . and he was also the poet of the East" (Diary, p. 785). Unlike the typical Russian intelligent, Pushkin managed to enter into and absorb European culture without losing himself in it.

Pushkin reconciles and harmonizes the two conflicting principles—Europe and the people—which have fragmented Russia's national identity. His works provide tangible proof for Dostoevsky of the Russian people's universality and their capacity for "eliminating contradictions" and "reconciling differences" (Diary, p. 785). Further, Pushkin's word has been productive and nourishing. Dostoevsky says that all subsequent Russian writers of value have emanated from him and have only "elaborated the tiniest part of the things indicated by him" (Diary, p. 785). In speaking of Anna Karenina, Dostoevsky says that its author "emerged directly from Pushkin," and in the Pushkin Speech he says: "It can positively be asserted that had there been no Pushkin, the men of talent following him would be non-existent" (Diary, p. 976).

Pushkin is one of the prime "facts" to which Dostoevsky points in The Diary in confirmation of his hope that "our destitute land will perhaps at length speak a new word to the world." Another such fact was the publication of Anna Karenina. Dostoevsky sees Tolstoy's novel as something that Russia can point to as evidence of her independence from Europe. He says "if Russian genius has proved capable of generating this fact, it is not doomed to impotence; it can create; it can give something which is its own; it can originate its own word and finish uttering it . . ." (Diary, p. 784).

From Dostoevsky's statements about Russia, Europe, the people, and literature, it is evident that the concept of nationality plays a crucial role in his view of history. Dostoevsky, like many of his generation, absorbed the ideas of the German romantic philosophers (Herder and Friedrich Schlegel) who held that each nation has its own absolutely unique genius which distinguishes it from every other nation and which makes comparisons between different nations meaningless. The national spirit (*Volksgeist*) represents, for these thinkers, the unifying essence of all the varied aspects of the life of a people and the source of its creative potential. The distinctive national spirit of each people is embodied in its language, which all the members of the nation share from infancy, and in its literature (above all, folk literature), which is the product of the nation's history.

The German romantics made use of the theory of the national spirit to resist what they regarded as the stifling domination of the French Enlightenment with its rationalism and its assumption of a single, universal line of development for all peoples. The doctrine of the *Volk* articulated the claim of all peoples to value independent of their level of historical development, by virtue simply of their irreducible uniqueness. Not surprisingly, this doctrine struck a sympathetic chord in Russia and contributed the fundamental assumption of both Slavophilism and populism. "Russia" could be substituted for "Germany," and "Europe" for "France"— the claim of the historically backward country to its own independent cultural life and to its own line of development remained the same.[32]

As early as 1861 Dostoevsky reacts against the Westerners who deny the existence of an essential Russian national character in much the same way he later reacted against the radical populists (Tkachev and Nechaev) who advocated the leveling of social extremes and the reduction of everything to a common denominator:

And there are those who are just on the point of discovering new laws, a general formula, for the whole of mankind, attempting to make a mold for some universal national form in which they wish to cast a universal kind of life without distinction of tribes or nationalities or, in other words, to transform man into an effaced copper coin.[33]

What is it that we love and know how to love in Russia sincerely, spontaneously, with all our being? . . . Is not the idea that we are a distinct, separate historic entity still considered as something shameful and reactionary by many people in our country? Do not the same people consider nationality, in the highest sense of the word, as something like a disease of which all-leveling civilization will rid us?[34]

. . . The Western ideals cannot be entirely accepted by us. They will never suit us, because they have not been the result either of our history or of our common heritage, because there were other circumstances that brought them about and because the right of nationality is stronger than any right that may exist among other peoples and societies.[35]

No nationality in the world, no state that is in any way stable, has hitherto ever been formed in accordance with a program recommended and adopted from outside. Everything living came into being and lived by itself.[36]

The last twenty years of Dostoevsky's life are marked by an increasingly intense adherence to this belief in the importance of the national principle and in Russia's universal mission among other nationalities. In *The Possessed*, written during the Franco-Prussian War, which he saw as a prelude to a final European conflagration, Dostoevsky has Shatov deliver a tirade on the subject of national identity:

"Science and reason have, from the beginning of time, played a secondary and subordinate part in the life of nations; so it will be till the end of time. Nations are built up and moved by another force which rules and dominates them, the origin of which is unknown and inexplicable . . . . The object of every national movement, in every people and at every period of its existence is only the seeking for its god, who must be its own god, and the faith in him as the only true one. God is the synthetic personality of the whole people, taken from its beginning to its end. It has never happened that all, or even many, peoples have had one common god, but each has always had its own. It's a sign of the decay of nations when they begin to have gods in common. When gods begin to be common to several nations, the gods and the faith in them are dying together with the nations themselves. The stronger a people, the more individual its god."[37]

Shatov goes on, however, to assert that "there is only one true god—the Russian." This assertion takes us beyond the claim of a backward country to equality with other nations as a distinct, unique, irreducible phenomenon. From his insistence on the importance of the soil (*pochvennichestvo*) and nationality, and from his program of fostering Russia's unique identity embodied in the people and their traditional institutions, Dostoevsky moves periodically to an aggressive nationalism, a vision of Russia's world-historical mission. The shift from a defense of the principle of nationality to an overtly political nationalism represents a shift from Herder, who rejected political nationalism and the idea that any nation was inherently superior to any other nation, to Hegel, for whom the Prussian state embodied the highest stage in the self-realization of the World Spirit.

Russia's peculiar identity and historical development have, Dostoevsky contends, destined her to play a world-historical role. Cosmopolitan Russia has understood and internalized what is most distinctive in each European nationality, and Russia will effectuate a synthesis among the warring nationalisms of Europe. Russia's future mission entails not just the reconciliation of the intelligentsia with the people, but nothing less than the transformation of Europe—the offering to a rotten, disintegrated Europe of a new ideal, that of universal brotherhood. Russia, it seems, can only manifest her full identity on a world scale. Dostoevsky's nationalism, it would seem, represents his most extreme attempt to resolve the contradictions of the Petersburg period, to gain recognition from Europe for Russia's individuality. The future, for Dostoevsky, holds the promise of the true "negation of the negation": Russia's alienation from herself which grew out of her cultural domination by Europe will be overcome only when Russia de-alienates *both herself and Europe.*

Dostoevsky's nationalism leads him to the paradoxical assertion that the Russian spirit is universal (*Diary*, p. 578). Russia's distinctive trait that will allow her to reconcile the conflicting European nationalisms is what Dostoevsky calls her "all-susceptibility," her sympathy with all peoples, her all-encompassing breadth (*Diary*, p. 979). Russia, which has come late to national identity and has been backward and secondary in relation to Europe, will, according to Dostoevsky, bypass the narrowness of European nations and achieve a higher form of identity—one which incarnates a universal humanity. Russia's nationalism, in contrast to European nationalisms, somehow transcends national distinctions and boundaries and unites that which is highest in different peoples. Her nationalism is a supernationalism. This dialectic reminds one of the logic of the proletariat's eventual triumph in Marx's scheme. Because it possesses nothing, because it is pure negation, the proletariat will become everything. It is the class which will abolish all classes. Similarly, Russia is the nation which will abolish all nations.

Another contradiction of Dostoevsky's nationalism is his claim that Russia is above politics and self-interest, that her overriding ambition has been and continues to be self-sacrifice and service to the West. Dostoevsky argues that Europeans cannot understand Russia's selflessness and maliciously attribute her behavior to self-aggrandizement. But it is certainly worthy of note that, in the name of Russia's higher mission, Dostoevsky extols the virtues of war (it brings together the Russian gentry and the people), of social upheaval (in Europe), and of annexation of foreign territory (Constantinople, Central Asia). Here, Dostoevsky himself seems to succumb to the logic of displacement, immediate transformation, and false mediation, which at other times he rejects as the very essence of the West.

It has been suggested that nationalism develops as a response to a wound, to a humiliation inflicted on a people,[38] and this thesis applies to Dostoevsky. His grandiose scheme of Russia's achieving ascendancy over Europe seems to provide him with a sort of psychic compensation for Russia's long-standing humiliation by Europe. This is strongly implied by Dostoevsky's refrain throughout *The Diary* that "Europe hates us" and "does not understand us" and by his exultation at the prospect of Europe's imminent collapse. Europe will be able to hear and understand Russia's "new word" only when she has been forced to acknowledge the bankruptcy of her whole historical development.

Dostoevsky's nationalism, along with his xenophobia and his anti-Semitism, reflect what I call his ideological side—that is, his tendency to resort to simple oppositions between absolutes in order to resolve complex problems. This tendency contrasts sharply with the attitude of mind in evidence in his fiction and even in much of his journalism, in which he is able to acknowledge the fears prompted by Russia's situation rather than denying them. In the last chapter, I will pursue the distinction between Dostoevsky's ideological and imaginative styles of thought. What must be emphasized here is that Dostoevsky's nationalism—and his ideological bent, in general—can be seen and understood as one response to the problems articulated in his view of history. It is an attempt to overcome the contradictions of the Petersburg period in Russian society and to assert the possibility of a strong, independent Russian identity. Dostoevsky's imaginative writings represent an alternative response to the problems raised by his view of history, and a different means of resolving the contradictions of the Petersburg period. But both have their source in a common world view.

3

THE IMAGINATION OF
SOCIETY

Indeed, by locking up the other person in a madhouse, one cannot prove
one's own intelligence.
                              —*The Diary of a Writer*

Why does he [the bourgeois] put all the poor people away somewhere and
insist that they do not exist?
                              —*Winter Notes*

Notes from the House of the Dead (1861-62) and *Winter
Notes on Summer Impressions* (1863) stand at the threshold
of Dostoevsky's last twenty years as literary records of his
encounter with the Other in its two most pressing shapes: the
people and Europe. Both works take as their subject something remote and novel to the Russian reader and examine it
in such a way as to implicate him, to point to hidden relations
between himself and the Other. In each case Dostoevsky
turns an account of a personal experience of another society
(he speaks of prison as being a self-contained society with its
own laws)[1] into a complex statement of general import about
Russian society. Both works record a descent into what is
described as hell, an attempt to understand its workings, and
both attempt to indicate the conditions for an alternative
society. What separates these two works from everything

Dostoevsky wrote before 1860 is a new sense of the density of the society within which the individual life is lived, a new sense of historical movement, and an urgency which this sense of history prompts. In Omsk and London, Dostoevsky discovers the ability of a social system to disfigure human beings almost beyond recognition. He learns that there is no Archimedian point outside society from which to transform it; the needed transformation can come only from within, from the application of the individual's energies not to some grandiose dream of total immediate (unmediated) transformation but to the slow, difficult task of self-mastery, of understanding the dialectic between the individual and the society, seeing oneself in the proper relation to others and overcoming the illusion of solitude, which is a socially fostered illusion.

In April 1849, at the age of 28, Dostoevsky was arrested for his participation in the Petrashevsky circle. This coterie of Petersburg intellectuals, university students, government clerks, and officials had engaged in discussions of French utopian socialism, especially of Fourier, and of the need for the abolition of serfdom. The group had been infiltrated by the security police (the so-called Third Section) and Dostoevsky was charged with having read aloud Belinsky's letter attacking Gogol for his apologetics for serfdom, the Church, and the autocracy. This transgression earned him a sentence of four years at hard labor to be followed by four years of service in the ranks. But before learning the actual sentences, Dostoevsky and the other Petrashevtsy were subjected to the famous mock-execution from which they were saved at the last minute by the order of Nicholas.

In the house of the dead at Omsk, Dostoevsky, the utopian socialist and Petrashevets, first became aware of the gulf separating the intelligentsia from the peasantry. For four years he suffered from the bitter hatred that the peasant convicts directed at the members of the upper class independent of individual qualities, and this experience forced him to reevaluate his early belief in the role of the intelligentsia in leading the people to a socialist utopia. Instead of being accepted as comrades by the peasant convicts, the political prisoners from the educated class were looked upon with distrust and hatred and with pleasure at their debasement.

In spite of the fact that they are deprived of all the rights of their rank and are put on exactly the same level as the other prisoners, the convicts never consider them their comrades. This is not the result of conscious prejudice but comes about of itself, quite sincerely and unconsciously. They genuinely looked upon us as gentlemen, though they liked to taunt us with our downfall. [IV, 26]

Even when educated convicts are stripped of the material attributes of their status, they remain outsiders by virtue of their education, their lack of the habit of physical labor, and their whole way of thinking. In the peasants' eyes they do not cease to be gentry upon being deprived of their rights and privileges. The peasant convicts do not believe in the "universal humanity" of the utopian socialists. They are viscerally aware of sociopolitical differences and they feel only distrust or disdain for any member of the gentry who tries to ignore those differences and make up to them. They are sticklers for form and want those in authority to behave with the dignity appropriate to their position. Any disregard for convention is taken by the peasants as an affront to their own dignity. In other words, they exhibit a hard-headed recognition of the way things are in the outer society and refuse to indulge in the illusions of the intelligentsia. Dostoevsky learns a lesson in class consciousness at the hands of the peasant convicts.

The impossibility of transcending their different backgrounds is brought home to the narrator in an incident which occurs toward the end of his ten-year sojourn in the house of the dead and which he recounts in the chapter entitled "Complaint." The convicts have staged a protest over the quality of the food they are forced to eat. When the narrator tries to join the protest he meets with ridicule and rejection:

"But why should you make a complaint?" he asked, as though trying to understand me. "You buy your own food."

"Good heavens! But some of you who joined in it buy your own food, too. We should have done the same—as comrades."

"But—but how can you be our comrades?" he asked in perplexity.

I looked at him quickly; he did not understand me in the least and did not know what I was getting at. But I understood him thoroughly at that instant. A thought which had been stirring vaguely within me and haunting me for a long time had at last become clear to me, and I suddenly understood what I had only dimly sensed. I understood that they would never accept me as a comrade, whether I were a convict or not, not even if I were in for life or if I were in the special division. [IV, 207][2]

The narrator says that this impossibility of joining the community of the peasant convicts constitutes the most painful part of imprisonment. The physical, external circumstances—the filth, the lack of privacy, the food with cockroaches in it, the chains—which were harder for a member of the gentry to accustom himself to than for a peasant, were secondary in comparison with the continual feeling of being an outsider, with the continual hostility directed at the gentlemen convicts by the peasants. The gentry prisoners were outcasts among outcasts.

No, what is much more important than all this is that two hours after his arrival, an ordinary convict is on the same footing as all the rest, is *at home*, is an equal member of the prison community. He is understood by everyone, and he understands everyone; he knows everyone and everyone considers him one of them. It is very different for the gentleman. No matter how straightforward, good-natured, and intelligent he is, he will for years be hated and despised by everyone; he will not be understood and, above all, he will not be trusted . . . . he will never be one of them and will always be painfully aware of his estrangement and isolation. This estrangement sometimes comes about without ill will on the part of the convicts, as if unconsciously . . . . They [the gentry] are separated from the peasantry by an impassable gulf, and this only becomes fully apparent when the gentleman is suddenly, by force of external circumstances, deprived of his former privileges and turned into a peasant. [IV, 198-99]

Notes from the House of the Dead is a record of the
narrator's (and, by extension, of Dostoevsky's own) attempt
to understand the peasant convicts with whom he is forced to
associate, who come from a different world.[3] His frustrated
desire to be accepted by them as a comrade becomes subli-
mated into a desire to understand them, to know what they
feel and what motivates their behavior. (He himself remarks
on the extreme curiosity which he develops: "I asked many
questions about the pain. I wanted to find out definitely how
bad the pain was, with what it could be compared . . . . I only
remember one thing, that it was not from idle curiosity. I
repeat that I was shaken and distressed" [IV, 153-54].) Finally, through the slow, painful process of gaining the beginnings of an understanding of his neighbors, he comes to accept them as different and yet to have faith that there are
explanations for their behavior even if these are inaccessible
and obscure; that they behave in the way that any human
being would behave if subjected to the same conditions. The
difference, then, the gulf separating the narrator from the
peasants which makes many of them almost unrecognizable
as human beings, is a measure of the deformation that human
nature will undergo under certain social conditions.

The peasants' apparent lack of remorse which so concerns the narrator throughout *House of the Dead* must be
taken together with other features of their prison behavior
which he calls attention to: their boasting and their desperate
attempts to lose consciousness by drinking, their deep longing
for freedom. In confronting these unfathomable "monsters,"
the narrator never relinquishes the intuition that he is witnessing the action of social forces on people who are (or were)
basically the same as he. It is as if he were witnessing the work
of erosion on a landscape and trying to imagine how certain
features were cut out of the rock. The peasants who at first
seem to have *their own* human nature pose a problem for
him and refer him back to the workings of society.

The narrator at times describes the most extreme of the

moral monsters he encounters as almost natural phenomena, limit cases beyond the pale of humanity and beyond comprehension. But often, after presenting what appears to be an insoluble enigma, he will himself provide a general explanation or will achieve a greater intuitive understanding of a convict owing to his increased sympathy for the convicts with the passage of time. In cases where the narrator reacts to a particular convict with revulsion, he gives us the context and indications for interpreting his own behavior, and we realize that his horror at a convict like Gazin or A——v is a metaphysical projection, an inability in a particular case to go any further in understanding what is before his eyes in terms of process, a failure of imagination. Such an abdication is doubly effective because it stands out as an exception to Dostoevsky's treatment of his material and it furnishes a symbol for the limits of sympathetic understanding. Here is what the narrator says about A——v, a convict from the educated class:

For the whole time I was in prison, A——v seemed to me a lump of flesh, with teeth and a stomach and an insatiable thirst for the crudest, most bestial physical pleasures. And to satisfy the smallest and most capricious of his desires, he was capable of killing and butchering in the most cold-blooded manner, as long as the crime could be concealed. I am not exaggerating; I got to know A——v well. He was an example of what the physical side of a man can become when it is not restrained by any inner standard or principle . . . . He was a monster, a moral Quasimodo. [IV, 63]

But this extreme description of A——v is preceded by the qualification:

Yes, it is very hard to understand a man, even after long years of acquaintance.
   This is why I could not see the prisoners at first as they actually were and as they appeared to me later. That is why I said that, even though I looked on everything with such a voracious and concentrated attention, still I could not make out a great deal that was right before my eyes. It was natural that I was struck at first by the

most remarkable and prominent facts, but even these I probably
saw incorrectly, and they only left me with an oppressive, hopelessly
melancholy sensation, which was greatly confirmed by my meeting
A——v. . . . [IV, 62]

Thus the narrator implies that behind A——v's degradation
there lies a story, a process, a history—that A——v is, in effect, human. His extreme reaction to A——v reflects his own
inability, at the beginning of his prison term, to see below the
surface. A——v, at any rate, is a special case by virtue of
being one of the few prisoners from the gentry. Not until the
writing of *Crime and Punishment* and the portrayal of Svidrigailov did Dostoevsky succeed in overcoming his revulsion at
a "monster" like A——v and in showing the emotions and
the logic which drive Svidrigailov to self-debasement. Significantly, in the process of humanizing A——v, the revulsion
that the narrator of *Notes from the House of the Dead* feels
for him is attributed to the moralizing Raskol'nikov.[4]

As for the peasant convicts, the narrator tells us continually throughout the *Notes* that he has studied them in vain
for any sign of remorse or repentance and this lack greatly
disturbs him. Yet his own copious description of their behavior makes this observation almost plausible. Early in the
book, he tells us that the convicts very rarely refer to their
pasts and to the crimes which have led to their imprisonment,
even though in general they make a display of vanity and
boasting in prison. How does one explain this silence if not by
a feeling of remorse? Still the narrator insists: "I doubt
whether a single one of the convicts ever inwardly admitted
his lawlessness" (IV, 13). He allows for vanity and false shame
in inhibiting the expression of remorse, but then concludes
that perhaps there was just nothing there, since throughout
his years there "surely it would have been possible . . . to have
noticed, to have detected something, to have caught a
glimpse which would have borne witness to some inner anguish and suffering in those hearts. But it was not there, it
definitely was not there" (IV, 15). In his search for an expla-

nation, the narrator focuses on the attitude of the convicts toward authority:

The convict is almost always disposed to feel himself justified in crimes against authority, so much so that no question about it ever arises for him. Nevertheless, in practice he is aware that the authorities take a very different view of his crime and that therefore he must be punished, and then they are quits. It is a mutual struggle. The criminal knows and never doubts that he will be acquitted by the verdict of his own class, the peasants, who will never, he knows, entirely condemn him (and, for the most part, will fully acquit him) as long as his offense has not been against his own people, his brothers, his fellow peasants. His conscience is clear, and in this he is strong and not morally perturbed, and that is the main thing. He feels he has something to lean on and therefore he feels no hatred, but accepts what has happened to him as something inevitable, which did not begin with him and will not end with him, but will go on for a long time as part of a long-standing, passive, but stubborn struggle. [IV, 147]

Thus, a partial explanation for the absence of remorse felt by the convicts is that they do not feel entirely responsible for their actions. Their "criminal" acts cannot be isolated from the "mutual struggle." They accept the oppressive system of prison and serfdom, lashing out only when things become unbearable, when "something snaps" (IV, 87). The narrator is struck by the lack of resentment and vindictiveness on the part of the convicts against their torturers and against those who, like the convict A——v, betray them to the authorities. The convicts have done away with external standards of judgment. Conventional morality is an abstraction and as such presupposes a certain distance from the acts one is judging, whereas for the convicts this distance no longer exists. They are completely at the mercy of the individual in authority over them at a given moment. Punishments are administered in doses which are just short of what would kill the prisoner.

In explaining both the origins of crimes committed by the convicts and their attitude toward crime, the narrator, above, refers to their feelings about those in power over them. The peasants could not feel remorse for crimes against those above them for the simple reason that a state of war exists between the two classes. However, there is another explanation which the narrator does not formulate but which follows directly from the reaction of various convicts to his (*as a member of the gentry*) probing for signs of remorse. When Orlov, the notorious robber who had allegedly murdered old people and children in cold blood, on being questioned by the narrator, realizes that the latter is trying to get at his conscience and to discover some sign of penitence in him, he looks at the narrator "with great contempt and haughtiness, as though I had suddenly in his eyes become a foolish little boy . . ." (IV, 48). This disdain along with the numerous references to the vanity and boastfulness of the convicts would seem to point to a certain self-consciousness and pride in their situation which does not allow them to show their deepest feelings, especially to an outsider. Their physical endurance under the lash which so impresses the narrator is thus equaled by their resistance to the expectations of the narrator. This second, implicit, explanation of the absence of remorse covers crimes committed by peasants both against authority and against members of their own class. The narrator always works on the tacit assumption that somewhere deep down even the most hardened criminal must feel remorse for his crime and that, if this remorse is hidden, that secrecy is an indication of the extent to which not only criminal acts but other modes of peasant behavior represent a reaction against oppression, an attempt to resist the impingement of the outsider's explanation of them and to preserve their freedom.

Their behavior, at any rate, confirms the narrator's contention that penal servitude does not awaken remorse in the criminal but, rather, militates against his experiencing remorse, since he feels further justified in opposing the society which punishes him.

In spite of the narrator's reluctance to pursue the roots of criminal behavior beyond the boundaries of the prison, he makes occasional reference to the outside, the larger society, and he repeatedly points to a determining relation between the prison and the society outside. The narrator makes these references as if in passing, but they invariably shed a glaring light on his often circumstantial and matter-of-fact account of prison life. Frequently, the implications of these passages are subversive, and Dostoevsky, having taken the line of thought as far as censorship would permit (one must remember that he had just returned from ten years of hard labor and exile!) breaks off with a rhetorical question and turns to another subject.

While discussing the "inequality of punishment" and the differing reactions among the prisoners to their lot, the narrator says:

And there are also men who commit crimes on purpose to be sent to penal servitude, *in order to escape from a far more penal life of labor outside.* There he lived in the deepest degradation, never had enough to eat, and worked from morning till night for his *exploiter;* in prison the work is lighter than at home, there is plenty of bread and of better quality than he has ever seen before; and on holidays there is beef; then there are alms and there is a chance of earning a little money. [IV, 43; emphasis added][5]

In another passage, the narrator remarks that: "These people are perhaps by no means so much worse than the *remainder* who have *remained* outside prison" (IV, 57; emphasis in original). Such oblique and seemingly inadvertent comments bring the reader up against the order of the society outside.

Furthermore, we learn that many of the convicts are in fact in prison for having attacked an oppressive officer when they were in the army. Dostoevsky does not draw attention to the fact, known to his contemporaries, that a certain percentage of peasants were recruited from each village into the army for a term of service which was 20 years on active duty plus 5 years of reserve duty in the militia until 1855, and 12 years on active duty and 3 years in the militia after 1855.[6] To these peasant recruits especially, prison must have appeared attractive. Conditions in the army were so grim that many young peasants mutilated themselves in order to avoid service. The narrator remarks of the prisoners in the military division: "Many of them returned almost at once to the prison for some second serious offense, this time not for a short term, but for twenty years: this divison was called the 'lifers'" (IV, 11). We further learn that the "special division" contained the most terrible criminals, principally soldiers (IV, 11). Orlov, the famous robber, was a runaway soldier (IV, 46). Petrov had stabbed his colonel (IV, 84). Luka had killed his major (IV, 90). The Kalmuck Alexander had killed his superior officer (IV, 145).[7] By presenting this background of the convicts Dostoevsky strongly implies that their "criminal behavior" stems from an intolerable situation outside the prison.

Dostoevsky provides an indication as to the process that leads to the seemingly senseless crimes of which he hears such grim rumors.

Some of the crimes were so strange that it was difficult to form even the most rudimentary conception of them. I say this because among the peasantry murders are sometimes committed for the most astounding reasons. The following type of murderer, for example, is met with often. This man lives quietly and peacefully and puts up with a hard life. He may be a peasant, a house serf, a workman, or a soldier. All of a sudden, something in him snaps; he can no longer contain himself and he sticks a knife in his enemy and oppressor. But here the strangeness begins: he loses all sense of bounds for a time. The first man he killed was his oppressor, his enemy; that is criminal, but understandable; there was at least a motive in that instance. But later on he kills not enemies but the first person he comes across, kills for amusement, for an insulting word, for a look, to make a round number, or simply "Out of my way, don't cross my path, here I come!" The man is, as it were, drunk, in a delirium. It is as though, once having crossed the sacred limit, he begins to revel in the fact that nothing is sacred any longer; as though he has an itch to defy all law and authority at once and to enjoy the most unrestrained and unlimited freedom, to enjoy the thrill and horror which he cannot help feeling at himself . . . . The more downtrodden he has been before, the more he itches to show off, to inspire terror. [IV, 87-88]

The prison authorities are sometimes surprised that, after years of leading a quiet, exemplary life and even being made a foreman for his good behavior, a convict for no apparent reason suddenly breaks out, as if he were possessed by a devil, and plays pranks, drinks, and makes trouble, and sometimes even goes as far as committing a serious crime—such as open disrespect for an officer, murder, or rape. They look on him and are amazed. And all along, perhaps, the sole reason for this sudden outbreak, in a man from whom one would least have expected it, is the anguished, hysterical manifestation of his personality, the unconscious yearning for himself, the desire to assert himself, to assert his crushed personality, a desire which suddenly erupts and reaches an intensity of spite, madness, mental aberration, fits and convulsions. So, perhaps, a man buried alive and waking in his coffin might pound on the lid and struggle to throw it off, though of course reason would tell him that all his efforts were useless. But that is the point: it is not a question of reason but of nerves. If we further take into consideration that almost every willful expression of personality on the part of the convict is looked on as a crime, then naturally it doesn't matter whether it is a small offense or a big one. If he is going to drink, he may as well do it thoroughly; if he is going to take a risk, he may as well risk everything and even commit murder. It is only necessary to begin. After that, he gets intoxicated and there is no restraining him. And so, it would be better, from every point of view, not to drive him to that point. [IV, 66-67]

Thus Dostoevsky reconstructs the logic that drives members of the peasantry to commit crimes so strange that "one could not form even a rudimentary conception of them."

If crime has its origin in the eruption of the repressed craving for self-expression on the part of the peasants, by implication the world outside the prison is not very different from the world inside from their point of view. They are desperate enough so that no consideration of punishment will deter them from giving vent to their "itch to defy all law." The grimmest irony of the penal system, as Dostoevsky describes it, is that the fear of punishment does not deter the criminal from committing an initial crime, but that once in prison the terror of approaching punishment actually prompts him to commit a second crime:

To put off the moment of punishment, as I have mentioned before, convicts sometimes resort to the most extreme expedients. On the day before his punishment, a convict may stab an officer or a fellow convict and get a new trial, thereby deferring his punishment for a month or two and attaining his aim. It does not matter to him that, when the punishment does come in a month or two, it will be two or three times as harsh, as long as he can put off the awful moment, if only for a few days, whatever the cost—so great is the prostration of the spirit in these poor creatures. [IV, 144]

The desperation of the peasant convicts and their craving for self-expression shows itself in drinking sprees, in which a convict will spend all the money he has saved for months, only to have to return to his weary routine the next day:

prison life is so dreary, a convict is a creature by nature so hungry for freedom, and from his social position so careless and reckless, that to have his fling for all he is worth, to spend all his money on drink, living it up with noise and music, and so to forget his depression, if only for a moment, naturally attracts him. [IV, 34]

The convicts' longing for self-expression also takes other characteristic forms. The convicts are continually exchanging clothes, food, and even prison sentences in their desperation to "change their luck," to escape from their immediate situation. The cycles of blind revolt and temporary suppression are intensified in prison, but they stem from the larger society, and the narrator repeatedly points to the world outside. I have cited his comment that there are men who commit crimes on purpose "in order to escape from a far more penal life of labor outside" (IV, 43). In one of the most powerful and intriguing passages in the *Notes from the House of the Dead*, the narrator discusses corporal punishment and the sadism of certain "gentlemen torturers." He has been speaking of the varieties of punishment administered *within* the prison, but it soon becomes clear that he sees brutal punishment as a symptom of the society as a whole. He has dealt amply with the attitude of the victim to punishment; he now turns to the effects of punishment on those in authority, and here he is talking about the educated class:

I don't know how it is now, but in the recent past there were gentlemen who derived from the power of flogging their victims a pleasure reminiscent of the Marquis de Sade and the Marquise de Brinvilliers . . . . Anyone who has once experienced this power, this unlimited mastery over the body, blood, and soul of a fellow creature, a brother in the law of Christ, anyone who has experienced this power and total license to inflict the greatest humiliation upon another creature bearing the divine image, will inevitably [ponevole] end by losing control of his own sensations. Tyranny is a habit; it has its own development, and in the end it develops into a disease. I maintain that even the very best of men can be coarsened and hardened into brutes by habit . . . . The man and the citizen are lost forever in the tyrant, and a return to human dignity, repentance, and rebirth are almost impossible. Furthermore, the possibility of such despotism has a poisonous effect on the whole of society; such power is a temptation. A society which looks with indifference on such a phenomenon is already contaminated at its very foundation. In short, the right of corporal punishment given to one man over another is one of the sores of social life; it is one of the strongest forces working toward the destruction of every germ of civic feeling and every effort on behalf of society, and a sufficient reason for its inevitable dissolution.

    The professional torturer [palach] inspires loathing in society, but a gentleman torturer [palach-dzhentl'men] is far from doing so. Only recently has the contrary view been expressed, and that only abstractly, in books. Even those who express it have not succeeded entirely in extinguishing in themselves the lust for power. Every factory owner, every capitalist [antreprener], must feel an agreeable thrill at the thought that the workman, with his entire family, is totally dependent on him. This is undoubtedly so; a generation does not quickly free itself from what it has inherited from the past; a man does not easily renounce what is in his blood and has been acquired, so to speak, with his mother's milk. Such rapid transformations do not occur. To acknowledge one's guilt and the sins of one's fathers is little; one must uproot the habit of them completely, and that is not quickly done. [IV, 154-55]

These forms of punishment, authority, torture, then, are endemic to Russian society as a whole; they are a product and a necessary correlative of the division of Russian society into two hostile classes. Not only is any form of self-expression on the part of the *convict* regarded as a crime by the authorities but any act of self-expression on the part of the *peasant serf* is also regarded as a crime. Prison represents not only the most extreme form of treatment of the peasant by society but the very essence of the peasant's position in Russian society— his lack of freedom. By using the terms "outcast" (*otverzhenets*) and "unfortunate" (*neschastnyi*) to refer to the prisoners, Dostoevsky calls into question the established view of criminality and consciously adopts the people's view. The word "outcast" refers to Dostoevsky's conviction that the purpose of penal servitude is not to reform the criminal but to take revenge on him and, above all, to remove him from society (and, of course, to deter others from making similar attacks). The term "unfortunate" is used by the peasants themselves to refer to the criminal not as someone to be excluded and punished but as someone in need of sympathy, someone who has suffered and brought more suffering on himself. For Dostoevsky, crime and the attitude taken toward the criminal are reflections of the order of society:

No, crime, it seems, cannot be interpreted from the standard, conventional points of view, and the philosophy of it is somewhat more complicated than is generally assumed. Of course, prisons and the system of hard labor do not reform the criminal; they merely punish him and protect society from further assaults on its security by the malefactor. In the criminal, prisons and the severest hard labor only inspire hatred, a thirst for forbidden pleasures, and a fearful levity. But I am firmly convinced that the celebrated system of solitary confinement achieves only false, deceptive, external results. It drains a man's vital sap, enervates, enfeebles, and terrifies his soul, and then holds up the morally withered, half-crazed mummy as a model of rehabilitation and repentance. Of course, the criminal, having rebelled against society, hates it and almost always considers himself right and society wrong. Moreover, he has already received punishment at its hands, and for this reason almost always considers himself purged and quits with society. From such points of view one is almost brought to justify the criminal. [IV, 15]

The convicts, although they do not show remorse and although they regard those in authority with hatred, reveal a deeper level of their psychology in their ability to respond to humane treatment. The narrator mentions repeatedly that the prison doctors show exceptional sympathy and humanity toward the convicts, playing along with their feigned ailments in order to allow them an occasional respite from prison life in the hospital. The convicts, in spite of their ingrained suspicions, respond to this humane treatment and we are told that they "never tired of praising" them. The peasants say of the doctors, "They are like fathers to us" (IV, 131). Furthermore, the peasants make distinctions even among officers in charge of punishing them. The narrator describes the convicts' reaction to Lieutenant Zherebjatnikov as opposed to Lieutenant Smekalov. The former is a sadist who "had something of the pleasure of an epicure in administering punishment."

He enjoyed it and, like the worn-out patrician debauchees of the Roman empire, he devised all sorts of refinements, all sorts of unnatural tricks in order to excite and agreeably tickle his fat soul. [IV, 148][8]

Zherebjatnikov's specialty consists of tricking the convict awaiting punishment into believing that he will take pity on him and then, taking the convict off guard, ordering the flogging with a vengeance. Smekalov, on the other hand, carries out punishments according to a particular fixed ritual which the convicts have come to expect. He transforms punishment into a game, into a joke which is shared by the convicts. Smekalov's method of administering punishment reveals his nature in general:

Smekalov knew how to make everyone accept him as one of themselves, and this is a great knack, or more accurately an innate faculty, which those who possess it are not even conscious of. It is a strange thing that some of these people are not good-natured at all, and yet they sometimes achieve great popularity. They are not squeamish or disdainful toward the people under their control—this, I think, is the explanation. You will not detect anything of the fine gentleman or the lord in them; they have a particular whiff of the peasant inborn in them, and my word! what a keen scent the people have for it! [IV, 150]

Smekalov, like the doctors, is referred to by the convicts as a father.

Another official who wins the affection of the convicts is Lieutenant Colonel G. The latter could not see a convict without making a joke or laughing with him, and "the main thing was that there was not a trace of a domineering manner in it, not the slightest hint of a condescending or purely formal kindness. He was their comrade and completely one of themselves. Yet, in spite of his instinctive democratic spirit, the convicts were never disrespectful or overly familiar with him" (IV, 215). The convicts refer to him, too, as an eagle and a father: "He is a father to us, a father! We've no need of a father!" (IV, 215).

To the narrator's surprise, the same convicts who ridiculed him for his ineptitude at physical labor and who hated him as a member of the gentry insist on his taking a front-row seat at the theatrical performance. Their hostility to the gentry does not prevent them from acknowledging and respecting the gentry's higher cultural level.

It seemed to me then, I remember, that in their correct estimate of themselves there was no trace of servility, but rather a sense of their own worth. The highest and most striking characteristic of the people is their sense of justice and their thirst for it. In the people there is no trace of the desire to be cock of the walk in all situations and at all costs, whether they deserve it or not. One has only to take off the outer, superimposed husk and look at the kernel attentively, closely, without prejudice, and some of us will see things in the people which we never suspected were there. Our wise men don't have much to teach the people. On the contrary, I can positively say that they should learn from the people. [IV, 121–22]

Observing the audience during the theatrical performance, the narrator sees: "A strange light of child-like joy, of pure, sweet pleasure shining on those lined and branded brows and cheeks, on those faces usually so morose and gloomy, in those eyes which sometimes gleamed with such terrible fire" (IV, 122–23). And he concludes: "When these poor people were simply allowed to do as they liked, ever so little, to be merry like human beings, to spend one short hour as though they were not in prison, they were morally transformed, if only for a few minutes" (IV, 129–30).

One of the narrator's descriptions of the "insolence of self-glorification" on the part of certain officials which "inspires hatred in the most submissive of men and drives them beyond their patience" is followed by the famous plea for humane treatment of convicts:

Every man, no matter who he is or how downtrodden he is, instinctively, unconsciously, demands respect for his human dignity. The convict knows that he is a convict, an outcast, and knows his place before the commanding officer; but no amount of branding or chains will make him forget that he is a human being. And since he really is a human being, he should be treated like one. My God, yes! Humane treatment can humanize even one in whom the divine image has long been obscured. These "unfortunates" need humane treatment more than others. It is their salvation and their joy. I have met kind-hearted, high-minded officers and have seen the effect they had on these downtrodden creatures. A few kind words meant almost a moral resurrection for the convicts. [IV, 91]

The narrator witnesses this kind of transformation during the celebration of Christmas in the prison. For this day the routine backbiting and boasting are suspended, and the convicts show dignity and reverence for the solemn occasion. Gifts are brought for the convicts from the town, and both rich and humble offerings are "accepted with equal gratitude, without distinction of gifts and givers" (IV, 108). The gifts are divided up evenly by the convicts without any quarreling or protest.

In addition to their innate reverence for the great day, the convicts felt unconsciously that by observing this holiday they were, as it were, in touch with the whole world, that they were not entirely outcasts and lost men, not completely cut off; but that it was the same in prison as among other people. [IV, 105]

The narrator of *Notes from the House of the Dead* attempts to uncover the kernel of human essence which has been obscured and buried by a system that disfigures both the oppressed and the oppressors. He tries to mediate between an existential hell and an ideal of human nature and of community which he catches glimpses of in the temporary transformations of the convicts. His narrative records his passage from alienation, resentment, withdrawal, and an instinctive feeling of superiority to a recognition of real differences between the peasantry and the gentry and to a firm faith in their common humanity. At the beginning of his term, as he tells us, the narrator developed an overwhelming hatred for his fellow convicts. Their hostility to him as a member of the gentry "became intolerable, poisoning" his whole life (IV, 176). It took him nearly two years before he succeeded in gaining the good will of some of the convicts. Looking back at that initial period, the narrator sees that his vision of his surroundings was obscured by his hatred and resentment.

. . . I did not, and indeed could not, penetrate the inner depths of this life at the beginning of my term, and so all its external manifestations were a source of inexpressible torment to me then. Sometimes, I simply began to hate these convicts who were sufferers just like myself. I even envied them and cursed my fate. I envied them for at least being among their own kind, having friends, understanding each other, even though, in reality, they were all, like me, sick and weary of this companionship under the lash and the rod, this compulsory association, and everyone was secretly looking for something far away from all the rest. [IV, 197]

I have already said that I was in such a state of mind that I could not even distinguish and appreciate those convicts who could have been fond of me, and who did become fond of me later on, though they never treated me as an equal . . . . I hated everything and I had no way of escaping . . . . In those days, I was sometimes so absorbed in myself that I hardly noticed what was going on around me. [IV, 199][9]

In the course of his years in prison, the narrator over-
comes his morbid hatred, envy, and feeling of isolation. The
initial resentment at not being accepted by the peasants is
gradually and painfully replaced by an understanding of the
peasants as individuals who in the last analysis elude all his
attempts at classification (IV, 197) and who yet appear to
him as not basically different from himself. In overcoming his
loathing of the peasants, in coming to see them as sufferers
like himself, as "sick and weary" as he was, and by gaining
some insight into their position in society, the narrator seems
to have broken out of the neurotic self-absorption which distorted his vision. His sojourn in the house of the dead has
opened up a world which could only be grasped by a leap of
imagination and by breaking down his delusions of grandeur.
For it is not unlikely that the Petrashevets Dostoevsky expected, if only subconsciously, some sort of recognition from
the peasants whose cause he had adopted and for whom he
was suffering in prison.[10]

Near the end of *House of the Dead* the narrator speaks
of his imprisonment as having afforded him the opportunity
to review his life and to judge himself sternly: "I thought, I
decided, I swore to myself that in my future life there would
be none of the mistakes and lapses there had been in the
past" (IV, 220). By penetrating into prison society and by
winning partial acceptance by the peasants, he has been renewed. His integration into the society of outcasts has drasti-
cally changed his understanding of society. At the very end of
the book, one detects in the narrator's tribute to his fellow
convicts at least an element of identification:

And how much youth lay uselessly buried within those walls, what
mighty powers were wasted there in vain! For one must tell the
whole truth: those men were exceptional men. Perhaps they were
the most gifted, the strongest of our people. But their great
strengths were uselessly wasted, wasted abnormally, illegally, irrepa-
rably. And who is to blame? [IV, 231]

One scene in *Notes from the House of the Dead,* the bath scene, stands out in most readers' minds above everything else. Turgenev, in a letter to Dostoevsky, referred to it as "Dantesque."[11] The scene provides the most powerful image of the contraries which are brought together for the narrator in prison and which must somehow be harmonized. Petrov, a criminal from the "special division" who had killed his colonel and who is regarded by the convicts as one of the most fearsome prisoners, escorts the narrator to the communal bath. Petrov looks after the member of the gentry as if he were a helpless child, as if he were made of china. He teaches him the complicated procedure of undressing and walking while wearing chains. Throughout the episode the narrator cannot account for Petrov's solicitude but allows himself to be directed by the peasant.

The bath itself strikes the narrator as a vision of hell. Eighty convicts are crowded on top of one another in a room twelve paces square.

Steam, blocking one's view, grime, filth, a crowd so dense there was no room to put one's foot down. I was frightened and wanted to turn back, but Petrov at once encouraged me . . . . it was dark, filthy, and a dirty slime almost two inches thick covered everything. But even the space under the benches was filled; there, too, the place was alive with human beings . . . . the dirty water dripped off them on to the shaven heads of the convicts sitting below. On top of the shelf and on all the steps leading up to it, men were crouched, huddled together, washing themselves . . . . Fifty birches rose and fell in unison on the shelf; they were all thrashing themselves into a stupor . . . . Liquid filth ran in all directions . . . . The shaven heads and the red steaming bodies of the convicts seemed more ghastly than ever. As a rule, the steaming backs of the convicts show distinctly the scars from lashings or beatings they have received, so that all those backs looked as if they were freshly wounded. The scars were horrible! . . . It occurred to me that if one day we were all in hell together it would be very much like this place. [IV, 98-99]

Petrov washes the narrator all over and especially his "little feet" even though the narrator would have preferred to wash himself. There is "not the faintest note of servility" in Petrov's attention to the gentleman narrator or in the use of the expression "little feet": "it was simply that Petrov could not call my feet just feet, probably because other real people had feet, while mine were still merely 'little feet' " (IV, 99).

What better image to sum up this problematic work? Guided by Petrov-Charon, the narrator makes his descent into hell, bathes amid the filth and grime and the press of convicts steaming themselves into oblivion; is supported, undressed and washed like an initiate in a rite of passage by a peasant who is unfathomable to him, who has murdered and yet is capable of the most gentle, disinterested solicitude toward a member of the gentry, without showing the slightest trace of servility.

In the summer of 1862, while *Notes from the House of the Dead* was appearing serially in his journal *Vremja*, Dostoevsky made his first trip to Europe. He had dreamed of visiting Europe ever since his childhood, when he had avidly absorbed the classics of European literature. Since then, Europe had played a decisive role in his political thinking both in his pre-prison utopian socialism and later in his *pochvennichestvo*.

The account of his ten-week trip, *Winter Notes on Summer Impressions*, allows Dostoevsky to ponder the central question of European influence on Russian culture. "To be precise, I was pondering the ways in which Europe has been reflected in us at different times and, together with its civilization, has gradually imposed itself on us as a guest; and finally, to what degree we have been civilized and just how many of us have been civilized" (V, 55).

Many articles on Europe had appeared in *Vremja* and other journals in the late 1850s and early 1860s,[12] and Dostoevsky had been amply primed with the view of Europe as torn by class struggle and dominated by a rapacious bourgeoisie. What makes *Winter Notes* valuable is that, in spite of Dostoevsky's polemical intent (reflected in the greater part of the book in his heavy-handed sarcasm), he was powerfully affected by what he saw in London and Paris, and *Winter Notes* records the intensity of his imaginative response to what he saw (especially in the chapters entitled "Baal" and "Essay on the Bourgeoisie"). Although the intention of the work is to show the difference between Europe and Russia, Dostoevsky dwells on the same mechanisms and syndromes which he had explored in the prison at Omsk and which, as we have seen, he interprets as symptoms of the state of Russian society as a whole. Also, the vision of London as a capitalist hell foreshadows the descriptions of Petersburg in *Crime and Punishment* and the descriptions of the power of money in Russia in *The Diary of a Writer*.

In his description of European society, Dostoevsky finds the same processes at work as those he had described in *House of the Dead*: the exclusion and abandonment of the poor, the outcasts of society; the erection of authority as something absolute; a deepening defensive self-degradation on the part of the outcasts (the cycle of drink, etc.); the attempt to break with oppressive authority in order to preserve the last vestige of their humanity; the reduction of the masses to the level of a herd, "systematically fostered loss of consciousness," their reduction to the level of dependent, helpless children. In other words, Dostoevsky's intense emotional response to the reality of London and Paris resonated with his experience at Omsk and his new insight into Russian society. Imagination grasps deep similarities. Ideology on the other hand posits differences a priori. (From his ideological position, Dostoevsky asserts that Russia is capable of a brotherhood that Europe cannot achieve. He ceases to be dialectical in his attitude toward Europe.)

Dostevesky sees the West as dominated by "a principle of individualism," a principal of isolation, of intense self-preservation, of personal gain, of self-determination of the I, of opposing this I to all nature and the rest of mankind as a separate, autonomous principle entirely equal and equivalent to all that exists outside itself. [V, 79]

In London, he finds

A city as boundless as the sea, bustling day and night, with the screech and roar of machines, railroads passing over the houses (and soon under them, too), that boldness of enterprise, that apparent disorder, which is, in reality, bourgeois orderliness in the highest degree; that polluted Thames, that air saturated with coal dust, those splendid squares and parks, those terrible parts of the city, like Whitechapel with its half-naked, savage, and hungry population. [V, 69]

This "bourgeois orderliness" consists in the intimate proximity of conflicting principles: "Each garish object, each contradiction coexists alongside of its antithesis and obstinately walks hand in hand with it, each contradicting the other but, apparently, in no way excluding the other" (V, 69). London presents the mystery of a whole made up of jarring, discordant fragments which seem to bear no relation to one another. Dostoevsky calls attention to extreme contrasts, between rich and poor, between the elegant, lamplit taverns and the derelicts who frequent them. These warring elements can presumably coexist side by side because of the "principle of individualism." Baal, the power of capital that presides over London, does not have to hide the poor as the bourgeois do in Paris. He does not suffer from anxiety as does the Parisian bourgeois. He is totally self-confident and triumphant. Thus he can accept the discordance around him. Out of the chaos of seemingly independent, clashing phenomena, the spirit of Baal makes a unity. Even the poor and the hungry bow down before the power of material wealth and worship it as the ideal.

Dostoevsky's reaction to London bears comparison with that of another visitor who preceded him by eighteen years— Friedrich Engels. Dostoevsky, like Engels, wonders at the force which draws people from all over the world to this city of "world-wide commerce" (V, 69). But unlike Engels, who scrupulously described the material conditions and the historical events (enclosures of commons, the expansion and concentration of landholding, the industrial revolution) which forced rural laborers off the land and into the factories, Dostoevsky conjures up the "colossal idea," the terrible force, the psychological principle that informs the experience of the material conditions and processes that Engels is most interested in.

Still, in spite of their different orientations, intentions, and habits of thought, it is striking how similar are the two men's descriptions of London. Here is Engels':

the inhabitants of London have had to sacrifice the best part of their humanity . . . *a hundred powers slumber dormantly in them, inactive and suppressed, in order that a handful of others might develop themselves more fully* . . . . The very bustle and tumult of the streets has something repugnant in it, something that human nature feels outraged by. Hundreds of thousands of people from all classes and ranks of society crowd by each other. Are they not all human beings with the same qualities and faculties; do they not all have the same interest in being happy? Must they not in the end seek their happiness through the same means and methods? Yet they rush past each other as if they had nothing in common, nothing to do with one another. They are in (tacit) agreement on one thing only—that everyone keep to the right of the pavement so as not to interfere with the crowds that stream in the opposite direction. Meanwhile it occurs to no one that others are even worth a glance. *The brutal indifference, the unfeeling isolation of each individual person in his private interest becomes the more repulsive and offensive, the more these individuals are packed into a tiny space.* We know well enough that this isolation of the individual— this narrow-minded self-seeking—is everywhere the fundamental principle of modern society. *But nowhere is it so shamelessly unconcealed,* so self-conscious as in the tumultuous concourse of the great city. The dissolution of mankind into monads, each of which has a separate purpose, is carried here to its furthest point. It is the world of atoms. [Emphasis added][13]

In this passage Engels brings together most of the ideas which Dostoevsky introduces in the chapter "Baal"; the suppression and sacrifice of the majority by the power of capital, what Dostoevsky calls the "systematic, submissive, fostered loss of consciousness" (V, 71); the extreme density of the population coupled with mutual indifference and isolation—the population of London forms "crowds that stream" but *mankind* is dissolved into "monads"; the writer's appeal to human nature and to outrage; the "narrow-minded self-seeking"—Dostoevsky's "principle of individualism"; and finally the lack of concealment ("Baal does not conceal from himself . . . the savage, suspect and troubling phenomena of the city's life . . ." [V, 74].

In another passage in *The Condition of the Working Class in England in 1844*, Engels speaks of the drunkenness he observes in Manchester:

Quite apart from all the usual consequences of drunkenness, one must consider that in these places men and women of all ages, *even children*, often mothers with babies in their arms, meet with thieves, swindlers, and prostitutes, who are *the most degraded victims of the bourgeois regime*. When one reflects that some mothers give spirits to children in arms, the demoralizing effect of frequenting such drinking places can certainly not be denied. It is particularly on *Saturday evenings*, that drunkenness can be seen in all its *bestiality*. *Wages have been paid*, the evening's enjoyment begins rather earlier than is usual on other days of the week, and *the whole working class streams* from its miserable slums into the main streets of the town. On such an evening I have rarely come out of Manchester without meeting many people staggering drunkenly about or lying helplessly drunk in the gutters. [Emphasis added][14]

Dostoevsky evokes a similar scene as follows:

I have been told, for instance, that on *Saturday nights* half a million workers, male and female, *together with their children, flood the entire city like a sea*, concentrating in certain sections, and celebrate the Sabbath all night, until five o'clock in the morning, that is they stuff themselves with food and drink, *like animals*, enough to last the week. *This uses up the week's savings, all that they earned with sweat and malediction.* Clusters of gaslamps burn in the butchers' shops and the eating houses, brightly illuminating the streets. It is as if a ball had been arranged for *these white*

Negroes. The people throng the open taverns and the streets. There, they eat and drink. The taverns are decorated like palaces. Everything is drunk, but without gaiety, morosely, despondently, and everyone is strangely silent. Only occasionally, swearing and bloody brawls disturb this suspicious and gloomy silence. Everyone rushes to drink himself into a state of unconsciousness . . . . [V, 70]

The two writers here call attention to the same phenomena and syndrome, but the tone and effect of the two passages are different. Engels is indignant, but his language remains abstract, somewhat formal and moralistic. Dostoevsky's language, on the other hand, is much more concrete. Although he appears not to have witnessed this scene personally ("I have been told . . . "), the power of his imagery makes the reader feel Dostoevsky as a participant in the scene. He creates a striking visual, almost tactile scene, as in the description of the bath, which is undiminished by any conclusions or moralizing. He is less eager than Engels to make explicit judgments about what he sees; one senses throughout *Winter Notes* a certain aimlessness, or free play (as distinct from a somewhat forced playfulness in the same work) as if he were constantly coming back to themes and images that fascinate him but that he doesn't quite know what to do with. He merely seems intent on capturing the brutality of the scene, and in order to do so he resorts to powerful imagery and contrasts.

At times the imagery of Dostoevsky's description of London explicitly echoes that of *Notes from the House of the Dead*:

Here, what you see is no longer a people, but a systematic, submissive, fostered loss of consciousness . . . . These millions of people, *abandoned and driven from the human feast*, shoving and crushing each other in the *subterranean darkness*, into which their elder brothers have cast them, grope for any gate at all to knock at, and seek an exit in order not to suffocate in the *dark underground*. This is a final, desperate attempt to band together in a heap, in a group of their own, and to break with everything, even with the human image, so as to be able to do as they please, so as not to be with us. [V, 71; emphasis added][15]

As in *House of the Dead*, the drinking sprees, the debauchery, the occult practices (Mormonism), the vagabondage of these "pariahs" are described as the last defenses against a colossal dominating force.

Curiously, this is the same kind of "irrational," self-destructive behavior that Dostoevsky argues will always be called forth by socialism (e.g., *Winter Notes*, V, 81; *Notes from Underground*). London, the center of the greatest industrial and financial power in the world, will remain for Dostoevsky the prime image of the human antheap in which the masses are compelled to exchange their labor and their freedom for material necessities. London appears to Dostoevsky as a frozen, stable society. History, and with it the possibility of human development, has come to an end there.

"Isn't this the realization of the ideal?" you ask; "isn't this the ultimate, the 'one flock'?" . . . you feel that something final has taken place here, that something has come to an end. This is like a Biblical picture, something out of Babylon, a prophecy out of the Apocalypse, coming to pass before your very eyes. [V, 69–70]

Here Dostoevsky uses the image of London to stand for the socialist utopia; it takes the place of the "enforced communism" of the house of the dead. It may seem strange to us that Dostoevsky should blur the line between capitalism and socialism, but for him the two are closely related both formally and historically. Both take the form of domination of the masses by a minority which claims to represent universal interests. Both are rigid and perpetuate the illusion that no further development is possible. The two are related historically in that socialism is, according to Dostoevsky, merely an attempt to replace the power of the bourgeoisie by the power of the excluded masses, an attempt to extend the myths of the French revolution to the majority of the population beyond the "one quarter" represented by the bourgeoisie.[16] Capitalism and socialism both represent the apotheosis of material wealth; they both rest on atheism. Socialism differs from capitalism for Dostoevsky only in the increased material security of the masses. But he sees this increased security under socialism as an even greater threat than capitalism, since the moral subjection of the masses and the elimination of freedom would be even more complete.

Thus, Dostoevsky's witnessing of the systematic dehumanization caused by full-fledged industrial capitalism in England provided him with his most intense image of the antheap, of the socialist utopia which is really a prison.[17] He will henceforth associate socialism with the London of the International Exposition and the Crystal Palace as in his arguments against Chernyshevsky in *Notes from Underground*. In other words, if Chernyshevsky, writing in the year after Dostoevsky's return from abroad, used the Crystal Palace as his image of utopia, this was unlikely to summon up favorable associations in Dostoevsky's mind.

A final feature in the passage quoted above on the masses "expelled from the human feast" which merits comment is the abrupt introduction of the pronoun "we": "to break with everything, even with the human image, . . . so as not to be with us . . . ." Here Dostoevsky seems to assimilate himself and his readers to the elder brothers who have expelled these pariahs from the human feast. The reading of literature presupposes education and leisure, which separates the bourgeoisie (or in Russia, the intelligentsia) from the workers who spend fourteen hours per day in the factories. Dostoevsky never lost sight of the fact that he was writing for a literate, cultured minority whose values were marked by their separation from the millions of illiterate peasants. Dostoevsky reintroduces the "we" at the end of *Notes from Underground*; it is both a device for implicating (if not accusing) the "reasonable" reader and a tacit acknowledgment on the part of Dostoevsky of the incongruous and problematic status of literature in Russian society.

If London is the capitalist inferno of the most advanced industrial state of the time, Paris incarnates the duplicity and hypocrisy which are the hallmarks of bourgeois society. In London, Dostoevsky was overwhelmed by the masses of pariahs flooding the streets and by the imposing monuments of industrial and commercial might which keep the hungry masses enthralled. The vision is apocalyptic, and with one important exception (the reasons for drunkenness) Dostoevsky pays little attention to psychology. He posits a force, a "presence of such hugeness," a "colossal pride" that goes beyond psychology and brings us nearer to allegory.

Paris, on the other hand, with its extreme individualism, calls forth a psychological and sociological essay on the bourgeoisie. Dostoevsky repeatedly asks what it is that the bourgeois is so afraid of. The bourgeois continually tries to impress you with his satisfaction with his lot, with the orderliness of his life and the stability of his enterprise. But at the same time, he is mortally afraid that he will be seen for what he is. In contrast to London, which strikes one by its glaring disharmony, Paris impresses Dostoevsky with its superficial decorum:

What orderliness! What prudence, what well-defined and solidly established relationships; how secure and perfectly delimited everything is; how content everyone is; how they all try to convince themselves that they are content and completely happy . . . . And what regimentation! Understand me: not only external regimentation, which is unimportant (relatively, of course), but a colossal, internal, spiritual regimentation, originating in the very soul. [V, 68]

This mania for decorum requires a psychological and sociological portrait to reveal what lies beneath it. The virtue and nobility that the French bourgeois lays claim to are simply the moral accompaniments of financial success. Money has become the source of all virtue, of all positive moral attributes:

To accumulate a fortune and to have as many possessions as possible—this has become the Parisian's principle moral code, his catechism. This was true before, but now it has an almost sacred character, so to speak. Formerly, he recognized something besides money, so that a man without money but with other qualities could count on at least a little respect; but now, none at all. Nowadays, one must accumulate money and acquire as many possessions as possible, and only then can one count on any respect. And not only respect from others, but even from oneself. [V, 76][18]

The slogans of the French revolution apply only to the ruling bourgeoisie, to the quarter of society that exploits the remainder as raw material. Dostoevsky asks: "What is *liberté*? . . . Equal freedom for each and all to do as they please within the limits of the law. When can a man do all he pleases? When he has a million. Does freedom give each a million? No. What is a man without a million? The man without a million is not one who does all that he pleases, but rather one with whom one does all that one pleases" (V, 78).

But the bourgeois has delicate feelings, and in his morality, law, and cultural life, his venality must be disguised as duty.

Ordinary stealing is vile and mean—it leads to the galleys; the bourgeois is ready to forgive much, but he will not forgive stealing even if you or your children are dying of hunger. But if you steal from virtue, ah, then you will be completely forgiven. You merely wanted to *faire fortune* and amass possessions, that is fulfill your duty to nature and to mankind. That is why the legal code clearly distinguishes theft with a base intention, that is, to obtain a piece of bread, from theft motivated by higher virtue. The latter is highly protected, encouraged, and is admirably organized. [V, 77-78]

Dostoevsky sees the bourgeois revealed most completely in the melodramas, which exalt, justify, and reassure him. In the typical melodrama, the threat to the bourgeois husband's marital harmony is eliminated by cooptation: at the end of the play the destitute, romantic lover always inherits money, marries, and himself becomes a bourgeois. Watching these melodramas, the bourgeois basks in the spectacle of his own magnanimity and relives the triumph of his order over all potential rivals.

The Parisian cannot live without melodrama. Melodrama will not die as long as the bourgeois lives . . . . Besides, the bourgeois possesses unlimited power today; power is his; and the miserable little writers of vaudevilles and melodramas are lackeys who always flatter those in power. That is why the bourgeois triumphs nowadays even when he is portrayed as ridiculous, and in the end he is always informed that all is well. [V, 95-96]

But the bourgeois remains ill at ease and afraid in spite of the justifications offered by his theater and morality. He is inexplicably insecure even though his triumph is complete.

Perhaps I was mistaken is saying the bourgeois cowers, that he is afraid of something. Not that he does not cower and is not afraid, but everything considered, the bourgeois is enjoying the utmost prosperity. Although he must constantly deceive himself and reassure himself that all is well, this does not in the least detract from his apparent self-confidence. And that is not all; even internally, he is terribly self-confident, when he gets enthusiastic. How all this can coexist in one person is a real mystery, but it does. [V, 85]

Psychologically, the French bourgeois manifests the same coexistence of conflicting elements which Dostoevsky observed in London.

The French bourgeois with his prosperity, his morality, and his culture is the model for Dostoevsky of divided, alienated European man. Referring to Sieyès' prophetic characterization of Third Estate, Dostoevsky points out that although the bourgeois is supposed to be everything, and indeed has become everything *politically*, he *feels* himself to be nothing. The bourgeois have a desire to "shrink into themselves, to change themselves into smaller coins, to shy away, to efface themselves" (V, 74). The bourgeois is not stupid, but he cannot see himself as he really is; "his mind is not penetrating; it is not systematic."[19] But there are reasons for his blindness, and Dostoevsky points to these succinctly and penetratingly when he asks: "Why does he put all the poor people away somewhere and insist that they do not exist?" (V, 75). In order to maintain his illusion that the rule of the bourgeoisie represents utopia, he must suppress reality, and this suppression takes a political form.

Although Dostoevsky emphasizes the differences in his impressions of London and Paris, he indicates a deeper identity, as if the contrasting aspects of the two cities are merely two sides of one coin. In both cities Baal reigns supreme. In both cities Dostoevsky observes the "same frantic struggle to preserve the status quo, to wring from oneself all one's desires and hopes, to curse one's future, in which even the leaders of progress do not have enough faith perhaps, and to worship Baal" (V, 69). Both represent a final ordering of society, an attempt to arrest history and to proclaim paradise on earth. Both cities, despite their apparently stable equilibrium, contain the threat of dissolution:

Yet, at the same time, one finds even here [in London] the same stubborn, smouldering, chronic struggle, the mortal struggle of the individualistic principle of the whole Western world with the necessity of finding some way to live together, of somehow creating a community, and setting up house all in one anthill; even if it is only an anthill, still we must get organized without devouring each other—or else we'll become cannibals! [V, 69]

Dostoevsky here seems to be expressing his own view of the dilemma of this terminal bourgeois society and yet borrowing the language of the socialists. This problematic passage indicates how closely the ideas of hell, utopia, and false utopias are bound up in Dostoevsky's thinking. After having characterized bourgeois society, he turns to the question of alternative organizations of society. First he characterizes his social ideal, and then he characterizes the socialist ideal. We shall take these up in reverse order since Dostoevsky's ideal seems to be formulated negatively, to a large degree, in reaction against the socialist ideal.

The socialists perceive the lack of equality and fraternity in society, but they believe they can overcome this lack by rational arrangements. According to Dostoevsky, they rely on reason to compensate for a lack in nature. But reason, he says, can only calculate advantages and obligations and appeal to personal gain, "determine what each person will look like and what burden each will represent; and determine in advance the division of earthly goods . . ." (V, 81). It can only fashion arguments, and arguments cannot replace the pre-rational, pre-reflective will toward brotherhood which has disappeared in the West. Arguments only tend to confirm the lack of a more solid basis for fraternity. Dostoevsky is convinced that a rational reorganization of society in which laws are imposed as something external upon a passive population will inevitably be experienced by individuals as constraint, as unfreedom:

> But this brings us to another enigma: it appears that the man is completely secure; they promise him food and drink, they give him work, and all they ask for in return is the smallest drop of his personal freedom for the common good, just one little drop. But no, the man does not want to live even on these terms, for the little drop is hard to surrender. It seems to him, fool that he is, that the community is a prison and that he would be better off on his own because he would be free. And though in freedom he is beaten, cannot find work, starves, and has no freedom at all, still this eccentric imagines that freedom is better. Naturally, there is nothing for the socialist to do but spit and tell him that he is immature, a fool and a baby, and that he does not understand what is in his own interest; that an ant, a mute, insignificant ant is more intelligent than he is, since in the anthill everything is so secure, so well delineated, everyone is well fed and happy, and everyone knows his task. In a word, man is still a long way from the anthill! [V, 81][20]

Fraternity will not come about in the West because "it is impossible to create brotherhood, because it creates itself, comes of itself, exists in nature" (V, 79):

> it must come about by itself, it must be present in one's nature, it must be an unconscious ingredient in the nature of the race . . . . in short, the desire for a brotherly community must be in a man's nature, it must have been born with him, or else he must have assimilated the habit through the centuries. [V, 80]

Dostoevsky concludes that the West cannot produce a society based on fraternity because fraternity presupposes a higher form of individuality. Only people who have attained this higher form of individuality can voluntarily and consciously sacrifice self for the benefit of all without outside constraint and without thought of recompense. "What would true fraternity consist of," Dostoevsky asks, "if we transpose fraternity into rational, conscious language?"

It would consist of this: each individual would of himself, without any coercion and without thought of personal gain, say to society, "We are strong only when we are united; take all of me, if you have need of me; do not think of me when you make your laws; do not worry in the least about me; I cede all my rights to you and beg you to dispose of me as you see fit. My greatest happiness is to sacrifice everything for you, without hurting you by so doing. I shall annihilate myself, I shall melt away gladly, if only your brotherhood will flourish and endure." But the community should answer, "You offer us too much. What you offer us we have no right to refuse, since you yourself have said that it would be your greatest happiness; but what can we do when our heart aches constantly for your happiness? Take everything that is ours, too. We shall struggle continually, with all our might, to increase your personal freedom and self-revelation. You need fear no enemies now among men or in nature. We are behind you; we guarantee your safety, we will watch over you eternally, for we are brothers, we are all your brothers, and we are many and strong. Therefore be tranquil and bold; fear nothing and count on us." [V, 80]

This is one of a small number of passages where Dostoevsky describes his social ideal. But it is less a description of a state than of a moment, the moment of inception of a new kind of society. Dostoevsky, who deplores the notion of rationalist social contract relying on self-interest, describes in effect the creation of a contract based on mutual self-sacrifice. But the actual state seems to defy description in words, except for one-word descriptions like "love" or "fraternity." Furthermore, the account of the creation of the contract—which presumably would take place spontaneously—is only a "transposition" into "rational, conscious language." That is to say, our habits of language and thought prevent us (the readers) from grasping directly what fraternity is. Dostoevsky attempts to express the idea of fraternity by means of a dialogue between the representatives of an individualism which is about to be superceded. But the speakers in the dialogue remain *on this side* of fraternity. In order for this conversation to take place and for the individual to "melt away" he must necessarily oppose his "I," at least momentarily, to the rest of society. And we still do not know what fraternity would consist of. One cannot translate from its unconscious source without running into paradox.

This brings us to Dostoevsky's belief that Russia can achieve fraternity, because in Russia only the relatively small educated class has been affected by segregation and loss of roots and identity. The people, the vast majority of the Russian population, remain uncorrupted and capable of fraternity. Dostoevsky identifies his utopia which is beyond words with the people who are untouched by culture or literacy and are thus also beyond words.

Konstantin Mochul'skii points out the imaginative and logical progression from Dostoevsky's discussion of the history of European influence on Russia in the first part of *Winter Notes* to the description of the "bourgeois paradise" of the Frenchman and finally of the capitalist hell of London.[21] We may also note a progression from a discussion of Russian patriarchal serfdom and its culture to a description of contemporary Western European capitalism, to a criticism of socialism, and finally to a definition of fraternity as the cornerstone of a new transcendent social order.

To weigh the significance of *Winter Notes*, after having read the "Essay on the Bourgeoisie" and the evocations of London and Paris one must retrace his steps and reread the discussion of the change Russia has undergone as a result of European influence. Here we realize that Dostoevsky is saying: "*De te res agitur.*" After describing the crude mimicking of European manners ("All this phantasmagoria and masquerading, all these French surtouts, cuffa, wigs, swords, all these chubby, clumsy legs slipping into silk stockings, all those soldier boys in German wigs and boots . . ." [V, 57]) indulged

in by the landed gentry of the eighteenth century and epitomized by Fonvizin's Gvozdilov, Dostoevsky declares:

Well, now things are different, and Petersburg has had its way. Now
we have matured and are complete Europeans. Now even Gvozdilov has got the knack; when it is necessary to let someone have it, he
observes the rules of propriety; he is becoming a French bourgeois,
and before long, he will be using Holy Scripture to prove the necessity of the slave trade, like the Americans in the Southern states. [V,
57]

And further:

The people already consider us absolute foreigners; they do not
understand a single word, a single book, or a single thought of
ours—but that is progress, if you wish. [V, 59]

In the eighteenth century, according to Dostoevsky, European influence was skin deep, a matter of snobbery, of following the fashions of the court. By the nineteenth century
European individualism, rationalism, and materialism have
penetrated the educated class. The gap between the people
and the intelligentsia has grown to the point where the latter
have become foreigners in their own country. How then can
the reconciliation between the people and the intelligentsia
which the *pochvenniki* so fervently called for come about?
The answer, as we saw earlier, lies in part in the intelligentsia's recognition of its 150-year estrangement from the people and what this estrangement has meant. Russians must
come to realize that their infatuation with the West was the
result of Russia's unique historical experience, that they
could never have become Europeans except by repressing
their historical identity. The alienation of the contemporary
Russian *intelligent* must be grasped in its full dialectic.

Dostoevsky's two-month trip to Europe both confirmed
his belief in the uniqueness of Russia's national character
(that uniqueness which he had discovered in the strength of
the peasant convicts in Siberia) and gave him a preview of the
future that Russia could look forward to if she continued to

follow the course entered on by Peter the Great with its consequent imitation of Europe and its promise of increasing social differentiation. If the Russian squire is being transformed into a French bourgeois and the *intelligent* is drawing even farther away from the people, Petersburg—"the most fantastic city with the most fantastic history of any city on the globe" (V, 57)—is in danger of becoming a capitalist hell curiously reminiscent of the London of *Winter Notes*.[22] And Petersburg seems inescapably to represent the future of Russia.

Like the populists, and especially Mikhailovsky, Dostoevsky reacted to the future as embodied by the industrialized metropolises of the West with their free labor markets and class struggles by looking to the Russian people, who appeared to him to have preserved more or less intact the conditions and beliefs necessary for the regeneration of society. Like the populists, Dostoevsky envisaged history as divided into three periods, the last of which would, after a period of transition, usher in a new Golden Age.

With the bourgeoisie there arose horrible cities which were never even dreamed of. Cities, such as sprang up in the nineteenth century, mankind had never seen before. These are cities with crystal palaces, with international exhibitions, banks, budgets, polluted rivers, railway platforms, with all kinds of associations—and around them factories and mills. At present people are awaiting a third phase: the bourgeoisie will expire and a regenerated mankind will come in its wake. [*Diary*, p. 417]

This sense of impending crisis and transformation—in Europe as well as in Russia—dominates Dostoevsky's later fiction both in the tone of the narrative and in the consciousness of the characters. The vision of society and its dilemmas held by Dostoevsky's most important characters and their fears and anxieties are very close to those expressed by Dostoevsky himself. The extreme "solutions" adopted by these characters, however, are shown up as magical, infantile acts which are inadequate responses to a complex situation. In his fiction, Dostoevsky's reaction to the dilemmas of the period of transition is less to offer any solution than to *represent* characters in the act of living and grappling with the crisis. He thus creates an imaginary space in which the consequences and implications of certain stances can be thought about.

4

THE ECONOMICS OF
WRITING

... Never in my life have I sold a work (with the exception of *Poor Folk*) for
which I have not been paid in advance. I am a proletarian among authors, and
if anyone wants my work, he must pay me for it beforehand. I myself condemn this system. But I have established it once and for all, and I will never
abandon it.
                                             —Letter to Strakhov, *Pis'ma*, I, 333[1]

DOSTOEVSKY'S DESCRIPTION, in his letters, of his situation as a
writer reveals correspondences with his other writings. The
themes of the obscure, formless present and the uncertain
future, the need for self-expression, and for creation of form
out of the fragmentation of the present are some of the basic
terms in which he describes his day-to-day existence. The letters provide an account of Dostoevsky's attempts to reconcile
oppositions he finds in his situation and the world around
him: between an intolerable present and a secure future, between his "poetic idea" and its "execution," between the material and the spiritual. In the letters we are not dealing with
unambiguous testimony, with objective fact, so much as with
Dostoevsky's perception of his circumstances and his deliberate heightening of certain effects for certain purposes. The
letters offer convincing evidence that Dostoevsky lived his
own life in conformity with his dictum that "Life is a whole

art and to live means to make an artistic work out of one-self."[2]

The letters, which show him taking stock of his situation, expressing his hopes for his writing, commenting on the tortuous process of creation, reveal Dostoevsky's strategies for dealing with adversity and pressing need. They abound in talk of money. They contain pleas addressed to friends and creditors for advances, promises of future works, descriptions of the cycle of dependence and debt that he is caught in, lamentations on his lot, and hopes for settling his affairs and for freeing himself from what he feels as an immediate and unrelenting external pressure to write. He is constantly forced to evaluate his work in terms of its monetary value, and at the same time he feels that writing to meet deadlines and for short-term payments forces him to rush and to mar his best ideas by inadequate execution.

Above all, for our purposes, the letters document the frustrations from which the imaginative work had to be wrested. On the one hand, the act of writing is an internal struggle to "embody" and express an imaginative idea; on the other, it is an activity dependent on the market and on a consideration of the public's and the editor's opinion. The letters show Dostoevsky trying to reconcile the conflicting demands of the material and imaginative realms.

The period for which we have the most letters is the four years Dostoevsky spent in Europe, from April 1867 to July 1871. I draw mainly on the letters from this period to give a picture of Dostoevsky's view of himself as a writer not because they are essentially different in tone and basic preoccupations from the earlier or later letters but because they are the richest and most powerful, owing undoubtedly in part to Dostoevsky's intense feeling of isolation from Russia and his friends.

His basic situation during these years can be outlined as follows: he has gone abroad with his new wife to escape his creditors, who are threatening him with debtor's prison. He is in foreign cities where he knows no one and where the difficulty of communication with his relatives, friends, colleagues, and editors in Moscow and Petersburg increases his feeling of isolation. In this situation he must write something "good," because his price depends on the success of his latest work with the public. Writing something good means allowing his imaginative ideas sufficient time to ripen and take the proper form, but his creditors continue to hound him. His health is poor, and this makes writing more costly and reduces his endurance. Furthermore, there are deadlines for Mikhail Katkov, editor of the *Russian Messenger* (in which Dostoevsky had published *Crime and Punishment*), and Dostoevsky is morbidly sensitive about missing a deadline because such failures weaken his position with regard to the editors and the public; specifically they weaken his credit. He lives on advances; thus he is never free to conceive a work without promising it to an editor or publisher, hoping to make enough money to pay back his debts and to attain a modicum of security, which would allow him to write free from pressure in the future. But producing a work merely renews his credit, which then gives him the courage to ask for new advances, which in turn require him to produce new works. He is always overextended.

In the letters we find a preliminary step away from the vertigo of extreme, intense experience, the first step in distancing, in Dostoevsky's creating of a persona and invoking the sympathy and admiration of his reader for his suffering and his surmounting of adversity. By representing his situation he gives it value and justifies his requests for money.[3] Thus the letters are in part a testing of his ability as a writer to communicate extreme experience. In this sense, his suffering and deprivation can always be turned to account, made productive.[4] The letters document the repeated movement from dispersion of self to a concentration of self, the movement toward self-mastery wrested from the dissolving flux of experience. This movement from dispersion, fantasy, the expectation of salvation from without, the desire to escape, toward an acceptance of his situation and the concentration of his energies ends for Dostoevsky in the act of creation.

Repeatedly, Dostoevsky emphasizes that everything, his whole future depends on the success of his current work. Work, writing, is a means of salvation, *a means of last resort, the one thing he can fall back on when his situation becomes impossible, unbearable, irremediable.* Writing is a paradoxical act in which his total dependence, his poverty, forces him back on his own resources (in his own words *"sosredoto-chit'sja v sebe,"* [*Pis'ma*, II, 33]), forces him, as Ortega puts it, to take a stand within himself (*ensimismarse*).[5] Total independence in one realm comes out of the acceptance of dependence in the other.

But before being able to fall back on his writing, Dostoevsky would periodically attempt to break out of his intolerable situation through compulsive gambling. He had a recurrent fantasy of winning at roulette that persisted for eight years, from August 1863, when he first gambled at Wiesbaden, until April 1871, when he gave up gambling for good. He had devised a system[6] which if he could keep to it would, he believed, assure him of winning. However, he would always lose his self-control, become excited, and lose all that he had won.

There is a dual motivation involved in Dostoevsky's gambling. He justifies it as a means of winning enough money to assure his future and that of his dependents; on the other hand, as he is well aware, money is a secondary consideration and what really attracts him is the sheer play (*"sama igra"*), the risk, the possibility of winning against great odds. Thus, in gambling he brings into opposition the material and the spiritual, financial and psychological utility. Gambling indulges Dostoevsky's fantasy of immediate, radical transformation, of instantaneous gain, of acquiring power by sheer force of will. The pure play comes from the gambler's collaboration with his will against chance, against the inertia and alienness of the material world. The gambler sets up an extreme opposition between his "I" and the most impersonal laws governing the external world with the hope of seeing the world give way, dissolve before his will. Gambling allows Dostoevsky to raise the stakes, to cast his situation in the most extreme, unambiguous form. By losing at gambling and thereby aggravating his situation, Dostoevsky is finally forced to take responsibility for it, to accept it, and to work gradually, continuously, to change it, to realize that for him there is no salvation outside of literature. The failed attempt at mediation (based on fantasy) allows Dostoevsky to proceed to the authentic and successful mediation of writing.

On May 21, 1867, after losing all his money at roulette in Hamburg, Dostoevsky writes his wife, who is in Dresden:"I shall free myself once again by work as I did three years ago" (before *Crime and Punishment*)[7] (*Pis'ma*, II, 13). Three days later, after losing again, he writes his wife: "I hate gambling . . . . I do not fear for myself. On the contrary, now, after such a lesson, I suddenly have become completely calm about my future. Now, it will be work and labor, work and labor and I shall show you what I am capable of" (*Pis'ma*, II, 18).

In reading these letters one cannot escape the impression that there is for Dostoevsky a profound feeling of release from anxiety and guilt when he has finally "lost everything," when "everything has collapsed" and when he has nowhere to turn but to his work.[8] The constraints of external circumstance (his financial need, editorial deadlines), as much as they weigh on him, count for little beside a more devastating internal constraint (fantasy) which takes possession of him and which is manifested most dramatically in his obsession with gambling. When Dostoevsky escapes for a time from this internal constraint by "losing everything" he is suddenly filled with a new confidence in the future. In a letter to his friend Maikov, written in August 1867 and referring to his recent gambling at Baden, where he spent seven weeks, he says:

I have always, and in everything, gone to the extreme; all my life I have overstepped the line . . . . gambling. Do you know how it consumes one? No, I swear to you, it is not only out of desire for gain, even though I needed money above everything else. [*Pis'ma*, II, 29]

On November 18, 1867 he writes to his wife from Saxon-Baden:

. . . I have lost everything, everything! . . . You can be certain that from now on I shall be worthy of you and shall no longer rob you, like a low, vile thief. Now, the novel, the novel alone will save us; if you only knew how much hope I am placing on it! You can be certain that I shall achieve my goal and will deserve your respect. Never, never again will I gamble. Exactly the same thing happened in 1865. It would be hard to fall any lower, but work has saved me. [*Pis'ma*, II, 55]

Four months later, again from Saxon-Baden, he writes telling her he has "lost everything." But this time he not only promises to work day and night but also emphasizes the positive and productive effects of his loss:

First of all, my angel, know that if it hadn't been for this sordid and vile incident, this vain loss of 220 fr., I might not have had the stunning, excellent idea which has just visited me and which will contribute to our definitive, total salvation! Yes, my friend, I believe that perhaps God, in his infinite mercy, has done this for me, a lost, depraved and vile gambler, in order to restore my senses and to save me and you and Sonja—all of us—forever from gambling. [*Pis'ma*, II, 105]

In order to placate his wife and to extract something positive from his loss, he lays out his saving idea which he is about to execute. The idea had already appeared to him even before his trip to Saxon-Baden, but "only vaguely" and never would he have put it into execution without this last "impulsion," "this shameful loss of our last crumb." "Now I will realize it." The terms Dostoevsky uses are the same he uses habitually to describe the process of writing: "idea," "execution" and the difficulty of making the passage from the former to the latter. The idea in this case is to write a letter to Katkov at the *Russian Messenger*—a confession—describing his personal situation in order to persuade Katkov to advance him 300 rubles so that he can finish *The Idiot* and pay back his debts. He will end with a declaration of dependence: "it is on you, Mikhail Nikiforovich, that my future depends!" "My fate is practically in your hands, Mikhail Nikiforovich"; and recalling Katkov's role in the past: "You have been almost Providence for me all this time, I shall say, and you made my happiness by helping me to marry a year ago. This is how I look on you" (*Pis'ma*, II, 107). He continues later in the same letter:

If you only knew how all this has suddenly calmed me and with what faith and hope I shall write the letter to Katkov tomorrow . . . . I feel so cheerful, so vigorous . . . . But formerly, although it had appeared vaguely to me, I still had not definitively understood this excellent idea which has now come to me completely. It came to me only at 9 o'clock in the evening or around then, when, having lost everything, I was wandering aimlessly in the park. (It was exactly the same as in Wiesbaden, when after losing, I invented *Crime and Punishment* and had the idea of entering into relation with Katkov. Either fate or God.) [*Pis'ma*, II, 109-10]

Three years later (April 1871), a trip to the roulette tables at Wiesbaden put an end to what he calls his "hideous fantasy" (*Pis'ma*, II, 348). It seems that he lost twice on this trip, since he tells his wife that he has lost the thirty thalers that she mailed to him for a train ticket, and in a postscript he refers to 180 thalers. In one of his recurrent moods of self-castigation coupled with a renewed certainty in the future, he says: "In the end you will see that this misfortune is not a cause for despair; on the contrary, something will be gained which will be much more valuable than what was paid for it" (*Pis'ma*, II, 345). Here again his lapse is the condition for a more precious acquisition which is not material and in the light of which the 180 lost thalers are "cursed and detestable" (*Pis'ma*, II, 349).

He tells his wife that he had renounced gambling for two reasons after losing the original 150 thalers: because of a letter from her which had "struck him" and because of a dream about his father which he had had the previous night: "he had the same terrible appearance with which he had appeared twice [before] in my life prophesying a horrible calamity, and twice the dream came true" (*Pis'ma*, II, 346). After renouncing gambling, however, he says that owing to the negligence of a post-office clerk, he was not given the thirty thalers in time for him to take an afternoon train back to Dresden and so made a last visit to the casino where he lost all but one and a half thalers.

He assures her that his fantasy is finished for good, that never before has he experienced the feeling that inhabits him now. He has been freed thanks to the dream, and if it were not for his anguish for her, he would bless the Lord for having arranged things thus, even at the price of a disaster:

Have faith that this is the last time, and do not repent. Now I shall work for you and Ljubochka without sparing my health; you'll see, you'll see, for the rest of my life, and I'll attain my goal! I'll make your lives secure. [*Pis'ma*, II, 347]

. . . it is as though I were entirely morally reborn . . . . A great event has taken place for me: the hideous fantasy which has tortured me for almost 10 years has disappeared. For 10 years (or more precisely since my brother's death when I was suddenly crushed by debts) I constantly dreamed of winning . . . . my hands were tied by gambling; but now I will think of work and not dream of gambling for entire nights as I used to. And therefore the work will progress better and faster and God will bless it . . . . I am renewed . . . . [*Pis'-ma*, II, 348]

Dostoevsky deliberately courted risk in his gambling. But writing, as he describes it, also involves risk and gambling. Describing the difficulties of work on *The Idiot*, he tells Maikov in a letter from Geneva of October 9/21, 1867: "In a word, I'm throwing myself into the novel head first; I have staked everything on this card; what will be, will be!" (*Pis'ma*, II, 47). In his next letter to Maikov, Dostoevsky who had just sent off the first part of *The Idiot* to Katkov, describes the infernal "torment" of having to produce "on demand." In this passage Dostoevsky characterizes the conflict between the demands of the creative process, or rather of thought in general, and the demands of external, mercantile reality (the system he speaks of in the epigraph to this chapter) in terms which recur throughout the letters. The passage is worth quoting at length:

Do you know what it means to *compose?* No, thank God, you do not. You have not written on command and by the meter and have not experienced this infernal *torment.* Having received so much money from *Russkii vestnik* (it's awful! 4500 rubles), I had hoped since the beginning of the year that poetry would not abandon me, that a poetic idea would appear and would develop artistically by the end of the year and that I would succeed in satisfying everyone. This seemed all the more possible since many embryos of artistic ideas are constantly flitting through my head and soul leaving their traces. But they only flit past whereas what I needed was complete incarnation which always comes about unexpectedly and suddenly so that it is impossible to calculate when it will occur; only after the image is completely formed in the heart can one broach the artistic execution. At this latter stage one can calculate without error. Well, I spent all summer and fall working on various ideas (some very involved) but experience has always enabled me to sense in advance whether an idea was false, too difficult, or nonviable. Finally, I picked one and began to work; I wrote a lot but on December 4th, new style, I sent it all to the devil. Undoubtedly, the novel could have been mediocre; but it repelled me beyond description precisely because it was mediocre and not *positively good.* That was not what I wanted. But what was I to do? It was December 4th! . . . In my letter to Katkov (thanking him) I positively assured him, on my word of honor, that he would receive the novel and I would send the editors a significant part of the novel in December (since the writing was progressing and I had written so much!). So I wrote to him telling him my expenses were very great and asking if he would send me only this once (for December) 200 instead of 100 rbs. out of the amount owing to me (500 rbs.). He agreed and sent the money in December just at the moment when I had destroyed the novel. What was I to do? All my hopes had collapsed. (My work, my novel was my main, my only hope; if I could write a satisfactory novel, then I could pay back my debts to the editors, to you, and send money to Pasha and Emilija Fedorovna [his brother's widow], and get by myself; and if I had written a *good* novel, I could sell the second edition, receive something besides, pay off half or two-thirds of the promissary notes and return to Petersburg.) But everything had collapsed. Having received the 200 rbs. from Katkov, I wrote assuring him that the novel would be ready *without fail* for the January issue and I apologized for being late with the first part. I said he would receive it *without fail* by January 1 (our style), and I asked him not to put out the first issue of *Russkii vestnik* without my novel (it never comes out before the middle of the month).

Then (since my whole future depended on it), I started to torment myself with the work of inventing a *new novel*. [*Pis'ma*, II, 59–60; emphasis in original]

After destroying the first draft (December 4) he spent December 4 to 18 thinking, and "elaborated on the average at least 6 outlines per day." He began writing on December 18, and on January 5, 1868, sent off the first five chapters of Part I of *The Idiot* to Katkov. The day before writing to Maikov (January 11) he had managed to send off the remaining two chapters, completing Part I. Thus he succeeded in rescuing himself and in keeping his promise to the editors. A week earlier (when he sent off the first five chapters) he had assured the editors that the second part of the novel would reach them no later than February 1 (n.s.) and that the third part was "almost finished." Now, he reveals to Maikov that he hasn't written one line of Part II. Pressure of circumstances had forced him to approach the idea for *The Idiot* before it was ripe, and again he invokes the comparison with gambling:

This idea had already appeared to me in a certain artistic form, but only partially, whereas total form was necessary. Only my desperate situation forced me to take up this unripe idea. I risked as at roulette, thinking: "Perhaps it will develop as I write!" This is unforgivable. [*Pis'ma*, II, 61]

But if writing for deadlines involves risk and negligence, Dostoevsky can at least assert that he is *honest* in literary matters,
and he insists on this repeatedly.

Questions of money are so intimately entwined with
writing for Dostoevsky that he feels obliged to explain that,
although he has always had to ask for advances from journals,
he never took money without having a clear idea of what he
was going to write. The future work has its own autonomous
logic which is independent of financial necessity. Dostoevsky's internal standard is independent of the "environment":

> But let me tell you straight that I have never invented a plot [*sju-
> zhet*] for money, in order to fulfill an obligation to meet a deadline.
> I have always committed myself and sold only when I already had
> in my head the theme which I really wanted to write on and felt it
> necessary to write on. [*Pis'ma*, II, 255]

In his next letter he says to Strakhov:

> I have always worked for those who give and gave me advances. It
> has always been so and has never been otherwise. It is bad for me
> from a financial point of view but what can I do! On the other
> hand, when I accepted an advance, I was selling something which
> already existed; that is, I sold it only when the poetic idea had
> already been born and had ripened as much as possible. I never
> took money in advance for a *blank space*, i.e., hoping to *invent* and
> *compose* a novel by the deadline. I think it makes a difference.
> [*Pis'ma*, II, 257; emphasis in original]

Thus the idea, once it has taken on a certain form in his
mind, becomes the guarantor of what is to come, of the finished work. Financial considerations surround Dostoevsky the
writer, but he insists that writing has its own internal laws and
demands which are, at least in the genesis and maturation of
an idea, unmotivated by financial considerations. (His destruction of the first drafts of *The Idiot* and *The Possessed* at
the last minute are dramatic instances of the autonomy of the
creative process for Dostoevsky.) The implication is that he
could never write just on an improvised theme. The idea is
born in a sketchy, unembodied form, and it must wait for

embodiment ("total incarnation") before he can write. By "write" I think he means "write the finished work." Certainly the process of incarnation took place largely through the writing of the plans and rough drafts in the notebooks. The actual writing, however, comes under the system of advances and deadlines, and Dostoevsky continually has the sense that he is mutilating his best ideas:

I am dissatisfied with the novel [*The Idiot*] to the point of disgust. I exerted myself terribly to work but couldn't: my soul is sick. Now I shall make a last effort on the third part. If I salvage the novel I will salvage myself; if not, I'm finished. [*Pis'ma*, II, 130]

I am tortured by the idea that if I had written the novel in advance, in the space of a year, and then spent two or three months recopying and correcting, it would have turned out differently, I assure you . . . . Now I see clearly as though through a crystal: I realize bitterly that I have never in my literary life had a better and richer poetic idea than the one which has occurred to me now for the fourth part. And what happens? I must rush with all my might, work without rereading what I write, run to the post office and, in the end, I still won't be on time. [*Pis'ma*, II, 141]

One could speculate that Dostoevsky thrived on the adversity of his surroundings—on the crudity of his creditors, on his dependence on advances from editors before whom he prostrates himself. Also one might cynically remark that his straitened circumstances and the external pressures on him afforded him an excuse for artistic failure. What is certain, however, from the letters is that his continual cycle of debt and deadlines forced him repeatedly into a situation in which he had "nowhere to go" and in which he had to write to "save himself," and that his extreme isolation and dependence on the market became a point of fierce pride with him and the mark of a distinction between him and his most eminent contemporaries, whom he refers to as producers of "landowners' literature."

I did not like Turgenev's *King Lear* at all. It is pompous and empty. The tone is low. Oh, landowners who have written themselves out! I swear I'm not saying this from envy. [*Pis'ma*, II, 300]

But if he does not envy Turgenev's recent output, he does, at times, express envy of the *situation* of the aristocratic writers, as well as anger at what he feels to be the insensitive treatment he receives from certain editors. Writing to Strakhov from Dresden in December 1870, he says:

But *if I were free*, i.e., if I didn't need money constantly, I wouldn't write any of the six [pieces] but would begin my future novel directly. This future novel [*The Life of a Great Sinner*] has already been tormenting me for more than three years, but I have not begun it *because I don't want to write it under a deadline but rather as the Tolstoys, Turgenevs and Goncharovs write. Let me write at least one work freely and not under a deadline.* [*Pis'ma*, II, 298; emphasis added]

In reference to Kashpirev, the editor of *Zarja*, to whom Dostoevsky, at work on *The Eternal Husband*, had made an urgent request for a second advance of 200 rubles, Dostoevsky writes to Maikov:

Did he think I was writing him about my misery for the beauty of the style? How can I write when I'm hungry, when I had to hawk my trousers in order to get two thalers for a telegram! . . . Can't he understand that I'm *ashamed* to have to explain all this to him? . . . He has offended me, offended me! Oh, how I would like to pay him back! Only *masters* treat their servants like that! As if I were some kind of clerk [*pisarishka*]! [*Pis'ma*, II, 219; emphasis in original]

And they demand literature from me! . . . And he, with the nonchalance of a landowner, answers my telegram on the twelfth day . . . . This is the negligence of a man who doesn't want to take notice of another's situation. Does he despise me *like a master* because I have gone through a month of such misery and have been in such *extreme need*! . . . Let him know that Fedor Dostoevsky can always earn more than he by his work! And after that they demand artistry, pure poetry, without signs of effort or tension and they point to Turgenev and Goncharov! Let them take a look at the conditions I work in! [*Pis'ma*, II, 220; emphasis in original]

It would not be fruitful to speculate as to whether, given more time and freedom from financial pressure like Tolstoy, Turgenev, and Goncharov, Dostoevsky would have, as he says, produced works in which the execution would have done greater justice to the idea which formed the embryo of a given work, nor for that matter to speculate whether he would have produced even less. What seems important is that Dostoevsky's statements about writing reflect a constant and painful awareness of the constraints and pressures of a publishing system which he finds irrational but which he accepts, makes use of for his own ends, and masters. He feels intense resentment at having to sell his second editions to merchants of literature for whom a novel like *Crime and Punishment* is a commodity, but he becomes adept at playing off one journal or publisher against a rival and letting them compete for his work; and although his thoughts about writing are intimately entangled in dependence on editors and on the market, yet he insists on the ultimate autonomy and integrity of the process of creation, on his freedom in the last instance from the pressures of the "environment." Here we can see the personal meaning of Dostoevsky's belief in man's independence of the environment (in opposititon to the positivists and utilitarians) and of his belief in the productivity of suffering. Dostoevsky does not deny that the environment affects people profoundly and even makes possible or rules out certain possibilities; but man retains an essential margin of freedom which is reflected in his ability to suffer. Writing, for Dostoevsky, is a continual assertion of his inner freedom, of his mastery, achieved at the cost of great suffering, over external, material necessity.

If the circumstances under which he is forced to write distinguish him from the landowning writers who, according to Dostoevsky, have the financial security and leisure to finish a work before sending it to a journal for publication, they also allow him to become the historian of the present as opposed to his rivals, whose novels portray a period that is rapidly passing away. Thus Dostoevsky implies a connection between his unusual situation as a writer, the subject matter of his fiction, and his ability to represent processes which are transforming society.

Since Dostoevsky repeatedly in the letters compares himself with the aristocratic writers of his generation both in terms of economic situation and in terms of the kind of literature they produce, it is strongly implied, if never explicitly stated, that a connection exists between his straitened circumstances and the kind of literature he writes. In other words, not only is his work affected in its "execution" by the pressure to produce for deadlines, but his fundamental conception of writing and the content of his writing are affected by his lack of financial security, his dependence on the market, his immersion in an unstable and threatening environment. He manages to create not only in spite of his adverse situation but also, and possibly in a deeper sense, *because of* his situation. If he feels himself subject to history in a way that the aristocratic writers are not, history in turn becomes the subject and ultimate concern of his writing. If he prided himself on discovering new patterns corresponding to new developments in society and producing them *on time*, that is, before or while they were taking shape, this talent owes something to his being in a situation which compelled him to *write* on time, for deadlines. In *The Diary of a Writer*, in 1873, Dostoevsky criticizes the preoccupation of the "artist recorders" of the Grigorovich school with the accurate recording of dialect and local color in the name of verisimilitude, to the exclusion of all other considerations:

our artists (like any group of commonplace people) are beginning to take sharp notice of the phenomena of reality, paying attention to typicalness and treating a given character in art when, in most cases, it has already passed out of existence or is vanishing, degenerating into some other pattern in accordance with the character of the epoch . . . . I will state that only an ingenious writer, or one endowed with a great talent, divines and produces a type *on time*; whereas triviality merely follows his path more or less slavishly, laboring in accordance with ready-made patterns. [*Diary*, 98; emphasis in original]

Dostoevsky constantly looked for, and usually found, confirmation of his prophecies, and the predictive power of his imaginative vision became for him the chief distinguishing mark of his fiction ("higher realism"). A typical example of his claim that actual events have confirmed his representation of reality in fiction appears in a letter to Ljubimov from May 10, 1879:

People reproached me for the fantastic nature of many of the characters in *The Possessed*, but later (would you believe it?) they were all confirmed by reality. So I had divined them accurately. For example, K. P. Pobedonostsev told me about several incidents with arrested anarchists which were strikingly similar to the incidents I portrayed in *The Possessed*. [*Pis'ma*, IV, 53]

Dostoevsky claimed to see new patterns and implications for the future in phenomena that appeared to be merely "exceptional" or "fantastic" to others. This ability to perceive the general import of incipient trends, before their significance was realized by most of his contemporaries, led him to formulate his distinct views on realism and reality:

Ah, my friend! I have completely different ideas about reality and realism than our realists and critics. My idealism is more real than their realism. Lord! If you recounted in a coherent manner what all we Russians have lived through in the past ten years in our spiritual development, the realists would shout that it was a fantasy! Still, this is venerable, authentic realism! This is realism, only deeper; theirs is shallow. Isn't Ljubim Tortsov [the central character in Ostrovsky's *Poverty Is No Crime*] a non-entity? Well, that is as much of the ideal as their realism permits itself. A profound realism, isn't it? With their realism it is impossible to explain one hundredth of the real facts which have actually occurred. But we have even predicted facts with our idealism. Yes, this has happened. [*Pis'-ma*, II, 150-51]

I have my own view of reality (in art) and what the majority calls almost fantastic and exceptional, sometimes constitutes for me the very essence of the real. The ordinariness of phenomena and the administrative view of them is, in my opinion, not realism—but the very opposite. In every edition of the newspaper you will find accounts of the most real facts and the strangest. For our writers they are fantastic; indeed they don't even pay attention to them; still, they are reality since they are facts. Who will take notice of them and record them? They are constant and everyday occurrences and not *exceptional* . . . . We let all of reality slip right by us. Who will preserve these facts and explore them? [*Pis'ma*, II, 169-70; emphasis in original]

In the above passages, Dostoevsky takes pains to distinguish himself from both the aristocratic writers who were roughly his contemporaries and from the *raznochintsy*, the plebian novelists born in the 1830s and 1840s (Pomjalovsky, V. A. Sleptsov, G. I. Uspenskii, F. M. Reshetnikov, etc.) who in the sixties produced sober, naturalistic accounts of the downtrodden and near-bestial condition of the peasantry. In a letter to Strakhov from May 1871, Dostoevsky describes the bearing of these two schools of artists, representing two different generations, on the state of Russian literature. The terms of this description directly parallel those of his descriptions of the state of Russian society in a period of transition. The old forms of society and literature have come to an end and the need for new forms is generally and pressingly felt, but these new forms are for the present inchoate. The aristocratic literature belongs to a former period (that preceded the emancipation), while the literature of the *raznochintsy* does not represent something that can take the place of the old as much as a symptom of the need for new forms:

All that is landowners' literature. It has said all that it had to say (and magnificently with Leo Tolstoy). But this culmination of the landowners' word was its last word. There is no *new word* which can take its place—and indeed, there hasn't been enough time. (The Reshetnikovs haven't said anything. But still, the Reshetnikovs express, even if in an ugly form, the inevitability of some new artistic word, no longer a landowner's word.) [*Pis'ma*, II, 365]

Dostoevsky combines the perspective and experience of the *raznochintsy* and their extreme sensitivity to the ills of the present with the creative powers and idealism of the aristocratic writers, whom he relegates to the past. It is this unique combination of heterogeneous historical traits which enables Dostoevsky to criticize the limitations of these two artistic movements and to see his own work as an attempt to utter a new word.

5

FANTASY AND FICTION

If a man is unsatisfied, if he hasn't the means to express himself and display that which is best in him (not out of vanity, but as a result of the most human necessity for realizing, establishing, and advancing his "I" in real life), then he immediately falls into the most improbable kind of condition; if one may take the liberty of saying so, he becomes a lush, or else takes to gambling or card-sharping, or picking fights, or goes out of his mind with ambition. . . . His vision is already so constructed as to see the fantastic in everything. . . . Imagination has been set up; immediately a whole story, a narrative, a novel is born . . . .[1]

IN APPROACHING Dostoevsky's fiction by way of his journalistic writings and letters, we can discern what Robert Jackson has called Dostoevsky's "movement toward form."[2] The gap between the scrupulous attention to the concrete detail of the present and the sweeping ideological assertions about Russia's future mission which we noted in *The Diary of a Writer* disappears in the fiction. In terms of this movement toward form, *Notes from the House of the Dead* and *Winter Notes on Summer Impressions* represent an intermediate stage between the journalism and the later fiction. These two works from Dostoevsky's immediately post-exile period have as their point of departure Dostoevsky's newly formulated faith in Russia's special mission and special identity. But here, by comparison with the journalism, we find an even greater degree of ambiguity and of evidence which undercuts Dostoevsky's ideological beliefs. Compared with the fiction, these two works are limited by the distance that accompanies the observation of an outsider and by a lack of the concentration that the subject matter requires. In *House of the Dead* and *Winter Notes* there is a certain rigidity, formality, and awkwardness. The reader feels that Dostoevsky has latched on to momentous dilemmas and fertile images but that he does not quite know what to make of them.

The letters can be read as an account of the arduous task of self-expression, of giving form to deeply held ideas. The letters make plain a central element in the structure of the novels which I will call the "life history of a fantasy." They point to the creation of the self-conscious characters of Dostoevsky's later fiction. These characters grapple with the dilemmas which Dostoevsky describes in his journalism, but at the same time they embody these dilemmas. They are creatures of fantasy; the alienation that Dostoevsky associates with the Petersburg period imposes itself on *individual* human beings in the form of fantasy. Consciousness of the dilemmas of Russia's history (such as Dostoevsky tries to foster in *The Diary of a Writer*) is, in the fiction, shown to be biased by distortions of consciousness. In other words, if fantasy is the ultimate result of Russia's historical alienation from herself, Russia's course cannot be changed by mere ideological assertion but only through the overcoming of fantasy in individual Russians.

The later novels are characterized by the confrontation of highly individual characters with momentous questions about society. In the protagonist of the later fiction a certain lucidity about the nature of society goes hand in hand with a blindness which stems from fantasy. The position of the *intelligent* protagonist—his marginality, his lack of connection, his "higher consciousness"—allows him a radical insight into the workings of society but at the same time condemns him to extreme, irrational behavior. This is the paradox of Dostoevsky's *intelligent*. The very individual who feels most called upon to change society is to the greatest extent its product; the "objective" observer who tries to predict the future is at the same time the frenetic solipsist of *Notes from Underground, The Gambler,* and "A Gentle Creature."

How can the preoccupations and patterns of the nonfiction be used to illuminate the fiction? Hopefully, our discussion of *The Diary of a Writer, Notes from the House of the Dead, Winter Notes on Summer Impressions,* and the letters allows us to supply part of the fiction's associative substrate. The historical schema which Dostoevsky developed in the early 1860s provided him with a conscious framework for interpreting events and a starting point for imaginative exploration. The central problems which preoccupy Dostoevsky in the nonfiction are the same as those that preoccupy his characters in the fiction. The main question of *The Diary of a Writer* is: How is Russia to emerge from its present—the "fantastic" Petersburg period—and to achieve an independent identity? In the letters, Dostoevsky describes his attempts to escape from an intolerable present and an intolerable fantasy and to achieve security and identity in his personal life. The fiction represents a continued exploration of these concerns.

This is clearest in regard to the *time* of the fiction. The fictional present coincides closely with the time of composition. The novels are, in other words, up to date.[3] The later fiction is thus situated in the post-emancipation period of transition, during which all the evils of the Petersburg period have intensified and in which the future is problematic. The problems of composition and of the form of the fiction reflect the dilemmas and disorder of the present. Dostoevsky makes this point by means of Nikolai Semenovich's comments on Arkadii's manuscript at the end of *A Raw Youth*:

"I confess that I would not like to be a novelist whose hero comes from an accidental family!

"To describe him would be a thankless task and can have no beauty of form. Furthermore, these types, in any case, are a current phenomenon and therefore cannot be artistically complete. One could make serious errors, exaggerations, oversights. In any event, one would have to guess too much. But what is a writer to do if he doesn't want to confine himself to the historical form, and is possessed by a longing for the present?"[4]

In situating the main action of his novels in the present, Dostoevsky confronts his characters with the same problems that beset Russian society and that preoccupy him as a writer, so that there is a basic equality between the writer and his protagonists. The setting of the fiction in the present emphasizes the urgency of finding forms and standards by which to explain contemporary phenomena and thus to conceive of an alternative. The expression of the ideal in literature along with the representation of the logic governing present-day Russian society appeared to Dostoevsky as a guarantee of the realization of the ideal.[5]

The protagonists of the later fiction tend to share Dostoevsky's view of the present as an obscure period of transition characterized by a frantic, competitive search for a foundation, for an ideal. They see themselves as "transitional creatures" standing on the border between two historical periods. The protagonist attempts to escape from what is felt to be an intolerable present, to change his situation, or to change the order of society. The present is perceived as hell, and at the same time the protagonist feels the possibility of harmony, community, utopia, paradise on earth. Desperate and isolated in the present, he pits himself against the whole society, which he wants to transform totally. But driven by his fantasy of immediate transformation, he reifies society and separates himself radically from it.

The protagonist (or maybe we should simply call him the *agonist*) is, in his purest form, an *intelligent* who has some powerful, lingering idea or experience connected with Europe: Raskol'nikov's obsession with Napoleon, and his theory cribbed from Napoleon III's *La vie de Jules César*; Myshkin's memories of Switzerland; Stepan Trofimovich's admiration of Goethe; Stavrogin's memory from the town outside of

Dresden, his four-year sojourn in Europe; Versilov's mysterious stay at Ems and his dream of the Golden Age; Arkadii's idolization of Rothschild; Ivan's nostalgia for Europe, his story of Richard, his Seville; Fedor Pavlovich's Enlightenment atheism; Smerdjakov's admiration of Napoleon and France; the gambler's attachment to Europe and Roulettenburg. Europe is associated with a certain investment on the part of the protagonist. The *intelligent* protagonist is distracted from the Russian present by his fascination with an idea derived from Europe or with an obscure European experience. Here we see a clear parallel between the fiction and the historical schema presented in *The Diary*, in which Russia's Petersburg period represents an "eccentric," "fantastic" interlude in her history.

Many of the characters in the novels give voice to or experience the intolerable suffering and injustice of the present and long for salvation. These characters, like Marmeladov and Snegirev, are descendants of Devushkin and Goljadkin. They suffer and lacerate themselves, but their desperation is always turned inward; they harbor no ideas in the sense of projects or programs, and it never occurs to them to confront society except by timid, token acts of defiance. The *intelligent*, on the other hand, who becomes the central character in the later fiction, feels pressed to act, to "realize his idea." The *intelligent* initiates the action of the novel, and the roots of his action lie in his idea. He represents a higher degree of alienation and fantasy than the other characters.[6] But he also has greater insight owing to his position as outsider. He sees the systematic nature of society, which the Marmeladovs do not see, and sees the rationalizations and illusions manufactured to perpetuate the status quo. At the same time, he enlists (exploits) the sufferings of others as justification for his withdrawal from society. His insight gives society a coherence, but it creates an even greater distance between himself and others. The discovery of the laws of motion governing society is coupled with the exclusion of oneself from society. The knower excludes himself from the known. The *intelligent* cannot mediate. His understanding is systematic but abstract. The objects of his thought become divorced from feeling. His understanding of society reflects his position—the distance separating him from the people.

The protagonist is an outcast, a loner, either an orphan or a child abandoned by its father. Upon reaching early adulthood he decides to launch his career, to break with the past, to claim his inheritance, to settle accounts with his father, his family, or the town in which he has grown up. He looks on the act of breaking with his past as the first, most decisive step in achieving his own identity; and this achieving of identity is confused with changing the whole of society. Although he insists on his total independence from society, he acknowledges his relation to it in a distorted form: he can only change himself by changing society.

The basic paradigm of the later novels can be summed up as an account of a "fantastic" attempt at mediation which ends in failure. The narrative of this attempt at mediation reveals the origins and the consequences of the protagonist's fantastic idea. The fiction is thus the life history of a fantasy and not of a particular character.

The notion of the fantastic present is central to the fiction. The period of transition is marked by real, historical oppositions which produced it (Russia/Europe; the people/intelligentsia; Slavophiles/Westerners) and which have become internalized in Russian minds as mental oppositions. In the historical schema, the Petersburg or "fantastic" period has its origin in Peter's turn to the West, in his rationalistic, modernizing reforms, in Peter's idea of transforming Russia on the European model. The protagonist of the later fiction, who is, of course, a creature of the Petersburg period, seems to recapitulate symbolically for Dostoevsky the essential features of the period. He looks down on the Russian people, he imitates a European model, and he desires to transform Russian society.[7]

Still, the protagonist of the fiction is more the victim of the Petersburg period than its originator. Here we come to another correspondence between the historical schema and the fiction. Peter's reforms created a split between the people and the upper class. The gentry came to look down on the people. They *abandoned* the people and this abandonment led to the deepening "segregations" and alienations which characterize Russian society of the present. In the fiction, as we shall see, the theme of abandonment is crucial in explaining the personality of the individual *intelligent*, who represents the extreme of independence and alienation from all social bonds. By means of the homology—gentry abandons the people; fathers abandon their children—Dostoevsky relates the life of the family to the history of the Petersburg period. This homology implies that the abandonment of children by their fathers is the final consequence of the division of society into two unequal groups.[8]

The abandoned, disinherited protagonist of the fiction, from the Underground Man on, seeks an object, a cause, an excuse for the way things are. He is obsessed with the past, and the past returns to him in the form of memories and dreams. But at the same time, he wants to make a radical break with the past and to begin a new life. The Underground Man is looking for a first cause, for someone to blame, and his principal gripe against the utilitarian "laws of nature" is that they eliminate the notions of first cause and responsibility and thus seem to undercut the justifications for anger and revenge. (It is of the utmost importance to see that the Underground Man is not motivated by some abstract objection to the laws of nature.) The laws of nature constitute for him a stone wall and there is nothing to do but:

"to sink voluptuously into inertia, thinking of how there is no one even to vent your rage at, that you can't find an object and maybe you will never find an object . . . ."[9]

". . . each question brings up so many more unanswered questions that a fatal mess, a stinking muck accumulates . . . ."[10]

". . . the responsible person is never found; the insult becomes not
an insult but fate, something like a toothache, for which no one is
responsible . . . ."[11]

As with all the *intelligent* protagonists, the Underground
Man's search for his place in the general web of causation
takes place within his blanket denial of continuity and relationship to his surroundings.

One can trace this search for a cause, for a person who is
responsible through the later fiction. Raskol'nikov latches on
to the pawnbroker as the perfect incarnation of a cause; Ippo-
lit and Budovsky blame Myshkin for their state; Stavrogin is
looking for an object to apply his strength to, for a faith to
justify himself, and for someone to confess to; Arkadii is looking for his father in order to understand his own origins; Mitja, Ivan, Alesha, and Smerdjakov are all looking for their father either to receive their material or spiritual patrimony or
to revenge themselves.

The later fiction reveals a progressive deepening of focus
in the object of the protagonist's fixation: from the secondari-
ness of the Underground Man's fixations on the officer and
Zverkov and Raskol'nikov's fixation on the pawnbroker to
Stavrogin's cosmic search for an antagonist worthy of him, to
Arkadii's and Ivan's fixation on their fathers.

In *A Raw Youth* and in *The Brothers Karamazov* the
relationship to the father emerges as the basis of society and
of identity. These novels investigate the question repeated
often in *The Diary of a Writer*: What can contemporary
fathers pass on to their children in the eccentric Petersburg
period? Lacking any "general idea" or ideal, cynical fathers
deny their children their rightful moral (and material) patrimony. This is the origin of the sons' fantasy of self-origination and claim to absolute freedom. The dual denial of relationship, on the part of fathers and sons, threatens the
continuity of society. The breakdown of inheritance from
one generation to the next, the symptom of the end of the
Petersburg period, is the ultimate consequence of the break

with Russia's past initiated by Peter. The fiction thus reca-
pitulates the historical schema and, more importantly, reveals
the workings of the past in the present.

The problem of Dostoevsky the artist is to supply missing links, mediations, explanations, that will fill the gaps between eccentric subjects each of whom is striving for totality,
for communion. The first step in establishing continuity is to
bring conflicting elements into relation, to accept discontinu-
ity.

Dostoevsky brings together individuals of higher consciousness who suffer from the awareness of their isolation. In
the Petersburg period *ideas* (fantasy) have taken the place of
direct, spontaneous participation in society. Ideas, as they are
held by Petersburg man, no longer serve the purpose of communication but rather intensify the individual's isolation by
giving him the illusion of completeness. Ideas totally dominate those who hold them. Shatov is described as one of those
"idealistic Russian beings who are suddenly struck by some
powerful idea which seems to crush them at once, and sometimes forever."[12] Dostoevsky reveals the origin of these ideas
and exposes them as substitutes for "living life." Extreme,
totalistic ideas have their origin in fantasy, abandonment, rejection, isolation, in the denial of a basic relation to one's
surroundings. The fantasist has withdrawn from the real
world, and from his vantage point of "total freedom" he attempts to forge a new society.

Dostoevsky takes as his self-avowed task the restoration
of man to man, the overcoming of fantasy by the elucidation
of its origins. As in the letters where he describes his compulsion to gamble and makes use of the excess of fantasy in
order to create coherent fictions, in the fiction he explores the
proliferation of fantasy, which is the psychological concomitant of social segregation, in order to create an image of eccentric society and to point to the possibility of renewal, and
the reintegration of the individual into a living community.

What Petersburg man fails to see is that isolation is a

relation; that he is conditioned by his history and his situation in society and that for this reason his fantasy of absolute independence is doomed to failure. By portraying aborted, unmediated attempts at total transformation, Dostoevsky is pointing to the need for mediation; the need for a notion of change which is adequate to his view of human nature. The novels provide a critique of fantastic notions of instantaneous change through the exhaustive examination of the effects of cetain ideas on those who hold them and on their neighbors. They provide a contextual, indirect, imaginative critique of these ideas—of their origins, consequences, and subsiding.

Dostoevsky reveals hidden and denied relations in the novels. He shows exhaustively how Raskol'nikov, Stavrogin, Ivan, and others are related to others in ways they cannot acknowledge. Beneath the fragmentation of society the novel discovers and asserts a vision of interrelatedness. Like Dostoevsky the gambler, who asserts his will one last time in order to reconcile himself to reality, Dostoevsky's protagonists oppose themselves to the world and to society with their rational egos in order finally to recognize, or to enable the reader to recognize, that they too are products of society and history.

Crime and Punishment

From the first page of this novel, we perceive Petersburg through Raskol'nikov's eyes, and later through the eyes of other characters, as a hostile, threatening environment. Like London, Petersburg summons up apocalyptic and infernal imagery with its Haymarket quarter crowded with the working poor, prostitutes, and beggars who drink themselves insensate, who fill the streets and taverns, who have essentially nowhere to go. While Raskol'nikov is filled with loathing at his surroundings and withdraws into himself, Svidrigailov has the detachment to note the "fantasticality" of the city:

"I am sure that there are many people in Petersburg who walk around talking to themselves. It is a town of half-crazy people. If we had any science in Russia, doctors, lawyers, and philosophers could conduct very valuable studies each in his own specialty. There are few places where one finds so many somber, harsh, and strange influences on the human spirit as in Petersburg." [VI, 357]

"The common people get drunk, the educated young people with nothing to do consume themselves with unrealizable dreams and fancies, and distort their natures with theories; Jews have flocked here from somewhere and are hoarding money, and all the rest pursue debauchery. I found the city reeking with its familiar odors from the very first moment." [VI, 370]

Women and children, along with the poor in general, are defenseless in *Crime and Punishment*. They are threatened with destitution and exploitation by the Svidrigailovs, Luzhins, and Alena Ivanovnas and have no one to protect them. Raskol'nikov's father is most significant in the novel for his inability to protect the mare from the drunken peasants in Raskol'nikov's nightmare. Raskol'nikov's dream refers not only to his plan to murder the pawnbroker but also to his desire to protect his mother and sister, and by implication Sonja and Lizaveta, all of whom are identified with the mare through the imagery of eyes and tears.

The need for protection recurs like a refrain throughout the novel. Raskol'nikov tells Razumikhin that Dunja must be protected from Svidrigailov (VI, 225). When Luzhin falsely accuses Sonja of having stolen 100 rubles of his, Katerina Ivanovna cries out: "Defend her! Why are you all standing still? Rodion Romanovich, why don't you take her part?" (VI, 305). Significantly, it is the muddled but sincere propagandist of utilitarianism, Lebezjatnikov, not Raskol'nikov, who intervenes to defend Sonja. On being evicted from her lodgings Katerina Ivanovna asks: "Oh, God! . . . Whom will you protect if not us orphans?" (VI, 311). And later, in the street where she and her children are begging, she exclaims: "when the Emperor drives past I shall fall on my knees, and put them all in front of me and point to them and say, 'Fa-

ther, protect them.' He is the father of orphans, he is merci-
ful, he will protect them . . . . Everyone has abandoned us!"
(VI, 329). Raskol'nikov tauntingly asks Sonja who will protect
Katerina Ivanovna's children when she dies (VI, 245). Marmeladov, at his first meeting with Raskol'nikov, tells the latter
of his failure to prevent Lebezjatnikov's beating his wife and
Sonja's taking to the streets. Svidrigailov tells the story of
courting his sixteen-year-old fiancée, who is at his mercy (VI,
369), and of taking an interest in a mother and her thirteen-
year-old daughter who have arrived in Petersburg without
money or acquaintances (VI, 371). These are all helpless victims with nowhere to go. They are in danger of being evicted
from their cramped rooms or "corners" and thrown into the
streets to join the crowds of drunks, prostitutes, and beggars.
Raskol'nikov says to Sonja: "Haven't you ever seen children
on street corners who have been sent out by their mothers to
beg? I know where and how such mothers live. Children cannot remain children there. There a seven-year-old child is depraved and a thief" (VI, 252).

Raskol'nikov is most active in intervening to protect a
helpless victim *before the murder.* Seeing a tipsy young girl in
a torn dress being followed by a fat dandy, he insults the
dandy and entrusts the girl to the protection of a policeman
with the words: "The main thing is to keep her out of that
scoundrel's hands" (VI, 42). After the murder, he watches
passively, as if in a dream, while a woman jumps off the para-
pet into the river (VI, 163).

The present is intolerable for Marmeladov, Sonja, Katerina Ivanovna, Pulcherja, Dunja, and Raskol'nikov. But Raskol'nikov is more concerned with the sufferings of others than
his own. He is, in large part, the helpless spectator who feels
compelled to act to change the way things are.

Raskol'nikov finds himself in an intolerable present. His
poverty, his dependence on his mother and sister, and his
physical surroundings—Petersburg in the summer with its stifling, malodorous atmosphere—all contribute to his sense of

desperation. He has withdrawn from all social intercourse, and as we see him on the opening page of the novel, his impulse is to avoid being seen by his landlady. In the street, after reacting with "an expression of the deepest loathing" to the "mournful and repellent picture" before him, he lapses into his habitual state of "willful unconsciousness of his surroundings" (VI, 6). He talks to himself, and we learn on the third page that he is absorbed by an idea. In the past month, this idea has taken on an increasing reality for him:

At that time, even he did not believe in the reality of his imaginings and only tormented himself with their ugly but tempting boldness. Now, a month later, he saw them in a different light and, in spite of all the monologues in which he deprecated himself for his lack of resolution, he had somehow, involuntarily, become used to regarding the "ugly" dream as a real project, although he still did not trust himself to carry it out. Even now he was *rehearsing* his project, and his agitation increased with each step he took. [VI, 7]

Of course, the rehearsal will lead in short order to the execution of the deed, to the dream's realization. But it is the fantastic nature of the deed and its meaning for Raskol'nikov that primarily interest Dostoevsky. The novel could well have grown out of an attempt to answer the question: How is one to explain a former student's murder of a pawnbroker to whom he had pawned his father's watch?

Raskol'nikov fixed on the idea of murdering the pawnbroker six weeks before the actual deed. He had just paid his first visit to Alena Ivanovna and had pawned a ring given to him by his sister when he overheard a conversation between a young officer and a student in a tavern. A "strange idea" had been pecking at his brain on his way home from the pawnbroker and now in the tavern he overhears a student propose that very idea. What are we to make of this use of coincidence and exteriorization of thought which plays such an important role in *Crime and Punishment*? In part, this particular instance points up the prosaic nature of Raskol'nikov's idea. It would seem to be a common fantasy among Raskol'-

nikov's contemporaries and the natural conclusion of the utilitarian ethic. Furthermore, Raskol'nikov, like the student in the tavern, will adopt the utilitarian justification for his act, even though from early in the novel he sees through utilitarianism as a rationalization of self-interest on the part of the oppressors (VI, 43).

Behind Raskol'nikov's project of murdering the pawnbroker lies a fantasy of longer standing: that of becoming an extraordinary man, a world-historical figure. Raskol'nikov had written his article in which he outlined his idea six months earlier, after leaving the university (VI, 198). In it he divides humanity into two categories: the majority of ordinary people who live in obedience to the law and who serve only for the reproduction of their kind, and the minority of extraordinary people who are capable of uttering a "new word" and who, because of their gifts, are not morally bound to obey the law (VI, 199). For those people, "everything is permitted" (VI, 211). Raskol'nikov presents his theory as an objective description of the basic dialectic of history, but Porfirii goes to the heart of the matter when he asks: "surely, it could not be, he-he, that you did not consider yourself, just a tiny bit, to be an 'extraordinary' person, one who was saying a *new word* . . . ?" (VI, 204). And, indeed, Raskol'nikov's project is to prove that he is extraordinary. He wavers between the two categories of his theory as he wavers between seeing himself as a louse or a Napoleon. He intends to murder the pawnbroker as proof of his extraordinary nature. It is a symbolic, magical act.

On the "practical" level the murder is meant to establish him by providing him with money to continue his studies and to help his mother and sister, who are sacrificing themselves for him. On another, "symbolic" level, the murder is an attempt to annihilate a symbol of the oppressive forces of a society in which money gives one power over other people's lives and in which lack of money means dependence on others. In this sense, it is an attack on the exploiters of society, the Luzhins and Svidrigailovs who threaten the defenseless and the poor. On a third level, the murder allows Raskol'nikov to identify with an idealized oppressor—a strong man (Napoleon) or a great man (Newton, Kepler) who can do what Raskol'nikov's father cannot do in the dream: that is, to protect a defenseless victim. On this third level Raskol'nikov hopes to achieve in fantasy what the money from the murder was to allow him to do in practice—to establish himself. With each of these levels, the act becomes more fantastic: the transformation that is expected to follow from the act becomes more inclusive, and the confusion between changing oneself and changing society becomes total. The money loses its importance. As in the act of gambling, it is "something else" that counts.

At perhaps the deepest level, the murder represents an infantile act in which Raskol'nikov is simultaneously the executioner, the victim, and the impotent observer, as in the dream of the mare.[13] The dream brings together the two perceptions of reality fundamental to Dostoevsky's fiction, those of the victim and of the rebel—the intolerable reality and the attempt to change it mechanically.

Raskol'nikov's theory with its binary oppositions is itself the product of his extreme isolation in his coffin-like room, of his conflict between fantasy and external reality. His attempt at mediation is a parody. The antithetical terms that he is trying to reconcile are not really independent entities; they are mirror images, and both have their origin in Raskol'nikov's fantasy. He cannot succeed in being either a louse or a Napoleon; he can only alternate between two equally fantastic views of himself.

Although Raskol'nikov repudiates the theories of the utilitarians and socialists, his act is based on an impulse which he shares with them, the need for an immediate transformation in the organization of society. With the socialists and utilitarians, the individual is swallowed up in the collective, whereas with Raskol'nikov society is swallowed up by his egoism, and he comes to confuse the transformation of society with his attempt to change his own situation. Razumikhin, in criticizing the utopian socialists, provides an unintended commentary on Raskol'nikov's motivation and on the nature of his act:

"For them [the socialists], it is not humanity, following the path of historical, *living*, development to the end, which will finally evolve into a normal society, but, on the contrary, a social system, originating in some mathematician's brain, that will instantly reorganize all of humanity and make it righteous and innocent in a flash, faster than any living process, without any historical or living development! That is why they so instinctively dislike history . . . . That is why they so dislike the *living* process of life: they have no use for the *living soul!* The living soul demands life, the living soul will not conform to mechanics, the living soul must be regarded with suspicion, the living soul is reactionary! But their social system, though it smells of carrion, can be made out of rubber—and it will have no life, it will have no will, it will be slavish, it will never rebel!" [VI, 197]

Raskol'nikov believes in the possibility of instantaneous change and in his theory he characterizes the majority of "ordinary people" as raw material, that is, lacking will or independence. He wants to join the pantheon of those who have asserted their will over the slavish masses. This, of course, anticipates the logic of Ivan's rebellion. In one passage Raskol'nikov unmistakably echoes the Grand Inquisitor and his fictional creator:

"Why do you say 'should'? There is no question either of permitting or forbidding it. Let them suffer, if they feel pity for the victims . . . . Suffering and pain are the inevitable lot of those of wide intellect and profound feeling. Truly great men must, I think, experience great sorrow on earth." [VI, 203]

Raskol'nikov, recognizing his affinity with the socialists' ideal, defends them mentally against Razumikhin's attack. He says to himself that he did not want to wait for the attainment of the "common good" while his mother went hungry (VI, 211). Thus he goes beyond socialism in his fantastic attempt to alleviate suffering. While he sympathizes with the goal of the socialists, he adopts the justifications and the means of the utilitarians whom he despises and takes this as proof of his baseness:

"I aimed at carrying out my plan as justly as possible, weighing, measuring, calculating: of all the lice, I picked the most useless and, when I killed her, I was determined to take from her only what I needed for my first step, neither more nor less . . . ." [VI, 211]

This "casuistry," as Raskol'nikov calls it, vitiates his attempt to demonstrate his extraordinary nature.

In his interviews with Sonja, Raskol'nikov, when pressed, retreats from one explanation to another, starting with the practical-utilitarian and moving to the egotistic (Napoleonic) and finally to the admission of his identification with the pawnbroker and his self-destructive urge. When he comes to the end of this tangle of motivations, he talks about his thoughts on change, and at this moment of maximum lucidity we see the relationship between Raskol'nikov and his alter ego Svidrigailov.

"Razumikhin works! But I became embittered and wouldn't . . . . Then, like a spider, I withdrew into my corner. You've been in my wretched little hole, of course, you've seen it— But do you know, Sonja, that low ceilings and cramped rooms crush the soul and the mind? . . . I should have been studying, but I had sold my books, and the dust is still lying inches thick on the notebooks and papers on my table. I preferred to lie and think. I spent all the time thinking. And all the time I had such dreams, all sorts of strange dreams; no need to describe them to you! But it was only then that I began to fancy that—No, that's not it! I'm getting it wrong again! You see, I kept asking myself: 'Why am I so stupid that when other people are stupid, and I know for a fact that they are, I don't want to be smarter than they are?' *Then I realized, Sonja, that if we waited for everyone to become smart, it would take too long. Then I saw that it will never happen, that people don't change, and no one can change them,* and it's not worth the trouble of trying!" [VI, 320–21; emphasis added]

"I did not commit the murder in order to use the money and power to become a benefactor to humanity. Rubbish! I simply killed; I killed for myself, for myself alone, and whether I became a benefactor or spent the rest of my life, like a spider, catching everybody in my web and sucking the life-blood out of them, was a matter of complete indifference to me at that moment! And most important, it was not money I needed, Sonja, when I killed; it was not the money so much as something else . . . .What I needed to find out, as quickly as possible, was whether I was a louse, like everyone else, or a man, whether I could overstep barriers or not!" [VI, 322]

Svidrigailov, the bored landowner and card-sharper, like Raskol'nikov, suffers from the loss of an ideal, and the lack of form that he sees around him. Like Raskol'nikov, he wants to break through to something solid, to some foundation. He wants to reconcile his desires with the world around him, and this spiritual kinship explains his deep interest in Raskol'nikov's experiment. Svidrigailov, like Raskol'nikov, is lacking an occupation, a place in society; he is unformed. But he seeks solidity in debauchery:

"In debauchery, at least, there is something constant, based on nature even, and not subject to fantasy, something that exists in the blood as an eternal flame, always ready to set one on fire, which will not be extinguished for a long time to come, perhaps for many years. You will agree that in its way it is an occupation." [VI, 359]

Svidrigailov is looking for "somewhere to sit." (VI, 358)

"Believe me, if only I were something—a landowner, say, or a father, an Uhlan, a photographer, a journalist—but I'm nothing. I have no specialty! Sometimes its even boring." [VI, 359]

Debauchery serves the same function for Svidrigailov as murder is intended to serve for Raskol'nikov. Both are attempts to break through to a reality that Svidrigailov and Raskol'nikov are cut off from. Both involve acts of aggression and provide the occasion for overcoming guilt and demonstrating one's superiority to "ordinary" people. Both men are self-made outcasts who feel that deviance is the only refuge for the extraordinary man and that change is not possible without violence and extreme self-assertion.

The spiritual void that Svidrigailov suffers from and which makes him undertake his "journey to America" is the counterpart to the physical and material hell that the poor of Petersburg inhabit. He is the product of the Petersburg period, incapable of work or of faith in an ideal. He is a prey to hallucinations, nightmares, and self-loathing. As he says, "The whole question is: am I a monster or am I myself a victim?" (VI, 215).[14] Svidrigailov has left his children with their aunt. He says: "What kind of father am I!" (VI, 222). A father who has abandoned his children and a young man who feels he has been abandoned (denied his inheritance) and is trying to protect his mother and sister and other victims of a cynical society.

Underlying his awareness of abandonment and exposure to a hostile environment, Raskol'nikov retains a picture of wholeness and security, an image of a Golden Age associated with the greater proximity to nature of nomadic peoples of the past:

He dreamed continuously, and very strange dreams they were; in the one that recurred most often he was somewhere in Africa, in Egypt, at an oasis. A caravan was resting; the camels were lying peacefully; all around, the palms stood in a perfect circle; the men were eating the evening meal. He was drinking the water from a stream which flowed babbling beside him. The water was so cool, marvelously blue, running over the colored stones and the clean sand with its gleams of gold . . . . [VI, 56]

From the other bank, far away, one could faintly hear the sound of singing. There, in the immensity of the steppe, flooded with sunlight, the black tents of the nomads were barely visible dots. Freedom was there, there other people lived, so completely unlike those on this side of the river that it seemed as if with them time had stood still, and the age of Abraham and his flocks was still the present. [VI, 421]

This image of a sensuous, warm, nurturative environment also appears to Myshkin, Stavrogin, Versilov, and to Alesha Karamazov (in his dream of Cana of Galilee). Like Pushkin's Aleko, who fascinated Dostoevsky, Raskol'nikov looks on the nomads with longing for a lost community and security. Freedom is there because freedom has not yet become a mark of distinction of the individual against the rest of society. Nature and man there form a continuity. There is no experience of absence, abandonment, exclusion, and the subsequent desire of Petersburg man to assert his freedom over others and take his revenge on society.

Raskol'nikov's fantastic act, which is meant to retrieve this lost state of innocence, is a betrayal of the dream image. His act is doomed to failure because it is meant as an instantaneous means of reaching a new state of being, a secure future, of creating something which, as far as Raskol'nikov is concerned, does not exist in any form. Raskol'nikov thinks that it requires an act of exemplary violence to bring about this new state, to utter this "new word." The fantasist does not realize that he contains this security deep within him and that what is necessary is only an act of rediscovery, of memory.

Raskol'nikov's magical act of transformation fails and, rather than saving his threatened mother and sister, puts them in greater jeopardy. He cannot eliminate the apparent embodiment of evil, Alena Ivanovna, without having to kill her half-sister and victim, who is associated with the very people he is trying to save and with the mare. Furthermore, it turns out that Svidrigailov is not the metaphysical embodiment of evil that the "Schilleresque" Raskol'nikov perceives him to be. Svidrigailov, like Raskol'nikov, is testing himself, and Raskol'nikov's experiment becomes important to him. As Svidrigailov remarks, they have something in common (VI, 224). Both want to know whether they have the right to take what they want. Svidrigailov's recognition of the ultimate futility of violence can be seen as the fruit of Raskol'nikov's experiment. Svidrigailov's designs are foiled not by Raskol'nikov's ax but by the sight of Dunja's helplessness and the repulsion she feels for him, and by his recognition of Raskol'nikov's failure to overstep the last barrier—that of conscience.

Raskol'nikov's failure paradoxically reveals a deeper unity than he had suspected. Nothing has changed, but for that very reason, everything has changed for him, and he can now enter into human ties. His fantasy is dispelled. He can now be open to "living life" and to gradual but real growth, "microscopic development." In his last dream, in Siberia, he sees his own fantasy as the disease which is ravaging Russia. He has stepped through the looking-glass. Raskol'nikov's denial of relationship, his assertion that "everything is permitted," can now be recognized as an aborted attempt to assert the value of human relations in a period and environment which seems to threaten their very basis.[15] Of course, he is not conscious of this. But the reader is, and perhaps for this reason sympathizes intensely with Raskol'nikov throughout the novel. Raskol'nikov's failure is productive because, in spite of his extreme and fantastic means, he senses what is missing and what is possible. Razumikhin's words apply ironically to Raskol'nikov:

"By pursuing falsehood you will arrive at the truth! The fact that I am in error shows that I am human. You will not attain to one single truth until you have produced at least fourteen false theories, and perhaps a hundred and fourteen . . . ." [VI, 155]

The failure of Raskol'nikov's attempt at immediate transformation, like Dostoevsky's failures at the roulette tables, causes the collapse of fantasy along with its absolute opposites. He can now accept his situation. His whole relation to his surroundings and to himself has changed. The failure of his attempt to achieve absolute freedom results in a new kind of freedom which he did not previously suspect. This is perhaps the sense in which Dostoevsky intends the words in the Notebooks to *Crime and Punishment*: "At the moment of the crime his moral evolution also begins. Now questions which did not exist before became possible."[16]

The Possessed

In *The Idiot* and *The Possessed* fantasy proliferates to threaten all of Russian society. It has been argued that these

two novels are closely related, and that their central characters, Myshkin and Stavrogin, are inverses, having a common
origin.[17] The failure of Dostoevsky's "positively good man" to
alleviate suffering leads to the examination of the negative
and destructive power by which Stavrogin dominates society.

In *The Possessed* Dostoevsky attempted to create a narrative around Stavrogin, the most mysterious and aloof of all
his characters. We know from the Notebooks for *The Possessed* just how tortuous Stavrogin's evolution was and to
what extent Dostoevsky, in addressing himself to the events
of the late 1860s, returned to his own political involvements
in the late 1840s. He confides in a letter that *The Possessed*
was the most difficult to write of all his books.[18] In the early
notes (300 pages worth) for the novel—which Dostoevsky destroyed in August 1870—Stavrogin occupied the foreground,
and his conflict between Orthodoxy and nihilism provided
the tension of the novel. The new plan which made it "necessary to change everything radically"[19] seems to have entailed
Stavrogin's withdrawal into the background as both the
source and the authority for the other characters.

Stavrogin is the focal point for the other characters' expectations and beliefs. He unites multiplicity with apparent
simplicity. But there is something complex, corrupted about
his simplicity. Stavrogin has apparently journeyed to the
source of contradiction. He lives at the moment of the inception of division, of the appearance of the red spider in the
original state of paradise. Stavrogin has an eye for the incongruous. Long before he appears in the novel, the narrator
notes that of all Stavrogin's impressions from his earlier stay
in the town,

the most sharply imprinted on his memory was the unsightly and
almost abject figure of the little provincial official, the jealous and
coarse family despot, the miser and moneylender who kept leftovers
from dinner and candle ends under lock and key, and was at the
same time an ardent believer in some visionary future "social har-

mony," who at night gloated in ecstasies over fantastic pictures of a future phalanstery the approaching realization of which, in Russia and in our province, he believed in as firmly as in his own existence. [X, 45]

This judgment of Liputin, as it turns out, coincides with that of the narrator (X, 430), but it also reflects significantly on Stavrogin's perception of the world. Stavrogin sees the gaping discrepancy between Liputin's actual self and his "fantastic pictures" of a future social harmony. The imagined phalanstery is the negation of everything Liputin represents yet it somehow leaves Liputin free in the present to be "a sharp man of business and a capitalist" (X, 430). The problem of *realizing* the future phalanstery does not occur to Liputin, and the problem of the continuity of the present with the future does not exist for him. Somehow he maintains this blatant contradiction in which the two opposed tendencies, far from hindering each other, enhance each other. The capitalist who indulges in Fourierist visions is free to be relentless in the pursuit of money.

Stavrogin recognizes something essential, typical, in the abject figure of Liputin. Stavrogin's preeminence in the world of *The Possessed* stems from his purified consciousness of the underlying mechanisms and contradictions of those around him. Kirillov says of himself that he cannot move from one thought to another as others do. "I can't think of something else. All my life I have thought of one thing" (X, 94). Stavrogin, by contrast, can best be characterized as someone who always thinks of at least *two* things simultaneously, and whose desire for any one thing is thereby diminished. This duality in Stavrogin can take the form of contradictory ideas which he entertains simultaneously; of an impulse and its inhibition; or, finally, of insight into contradiction in the world around him (as in his reaction to Liputin). Stavrogin hovers at the edge of negation, he concentrates his formidable strength on the act of restraining his anger at Shatov's blow. When Kirillov tells Stavrogin of his plan to shoot himself, Stavrogin responds: "I sometimes have thought of it myself, and then there always came a new idea: if one did something wicked . . ." (X, 187). The incident that Stavrogin relates at the beginning of his confession provides a concise image of his esthetic cultivation of incongruity:

"I rented both my other apartments by the month for love affairs; in one I received a certain lady who loved me and in the other her maid, and for a while I was very much preoccupied with the effort to bring them both together so that the lady and the girl would meet at my place in front of my friends and her husband." [XI, 12-13]

This two-timing of Stavrogin's resembles his two-timing of Kirillov and Shatov. Stavrogin supplied both Kirillov and Shatov with their contradictory and all-consuming ideas at the same time (X, 197). The implication is that Stavrogin, in his search for a foundation, can entertain two such ideas simultaneously and that it is precisely the contrast between them that titillates him.

This duality accounts for Stavrogin's haunting depth. He is the victim of a truncated dialectic. For every impulse there is a counter-impulse, for every idea a counter-idea. There is no synthesis. The conflict is carried over from one situation to another with alternatives always resolving themselves into oppositions. Stavrogin's inner division is symbolized most importantly in his reflexiveness, his interior distance. Kirillov formulates this point forcefully when he says: "if Stavrogin believes, he does not believe that he believes. If he doesn't believe, he does not believe that he doesn't" (X, 469). Stavrogin's life is a continual process of deepening internalization marked by inhibited impulses on top of inhibited impulses. He appears static, cold, and indifferent only from without. Actually the process of self-control requires continual work.

Stavrogin's ultimate act of negation is his confusion of the thirteen-year-old Matresha, which he relates in his confession. By evoking fear and affection by turns, he creates division in Matresha and drives her to suicide. This crime, which

Stavrogin committed five years before his last visit to town, dominates his subsequent behavior. His marriage to Mar'ja Lebjadkina followed the decision to mutilate his life because of the event on Gorokhovaja Street which he "remembered with fury" (XI, 20). Stavrogin's subsequent search for a faith, which takes him to Jerusalem, Mount Athos, Iceland, and Göttingen and which leaves behind his progeny possessed each by a particular idea like so many skins sloughed off by a snake, has as its point of departure the murder of Matresha.[20]

The dream of the golden age, or primal unity is blotted out by Stavrogin's crime. Stavrogin's subsequent search for faith is directed at overcoming the intolerable division, the separateness of the present, in order to regain this archaic state of harmony. But all the ideas which he bequeathes to his epigones bear the mark of their origin. All the ideas formulated by Stavrogin point to a desideratum without specifying the means commensurate with the ideal. All the ideas entail a stark contradiction or discrepancy. Shigalev says of his theory: "I am perplexed by my own data, and my conclusion is a direct contradiction of the original idea with which I start. Starting from unlimited freedom, I arrive at unlimited despotism" (X, 311). Kirillov arrives at the grisly paradox of demonstrating his freedom while Petr Verkhovenskii waits, pistol in hand, to make sure he finishes the job. Kirillov expresses his paradox in the following words: ". . . I am bound to show self-will" (X, 470); ". . . I am bound to believe that I don't believe" (X, 472). Shatov, who preaches the god-bearing mission of the Russian people, does not yet himself have faith in God. Petr Verkhovenskii wants to reduce Russia to chaos, "to level the mountains" in preparation for a new and as yet unconceived era, but his vast organizational network rests on a confidence trick and contains probably no more than one "group of five." Stavrogin, his reluctant source of inspiration, deserts him, and Petr remains "a Columbus without an America" (X, 326).

The Possessed marks the apogee in Dostoevsky's later

novels of the proliferation of fantasy and delusion. Almost every character in this novel looks forward to an impending, immediate transformation in his life or in society. Lebjadkin, Mar'ja Lebjadkina, Fed'ka, Shatov, Kirillov, Petr Verkhovenskii, Varvara Stavrogina, Liza, Dasha, Stepan Trofimovich have all been "waiting" for Stavrogin and expecting him to fulfill their deep longing. The whole town is "fascinated" with Stavrogin. Many of the characters have the fantasy of forming a group around themselves which will provide a new model for society: Julija von Lembke, Stepan Trofimovich, Varvara Stavrogina, Shatov, Kirillov, Shigalev, Petr Verkhovenskii. *The Possessed* portrays frantic, deluded individuals attempting to transform a fragmented society into a unified whole. What is lacking both in the isolated individuals and in the ideas they latch onto is some sense of continuity or communality. The radical division which Stavrogin marvels at in Liputin pervades every member of this society and attains its fullest elaboration in Stavrogin himself. There is what J. Hillis Miller, writing about Conrad's *The Secret Agent*, has called a "sinister connectedness of all levels of society from top to bottom, from the far left to the far right."[21] The nihilist Petr Verkhovenskii and the impotent governor Von Lembke realize how close they stand to each other, how each requires the other (X, 245-46). As in *Dead Souls*, the characters in *The Possessed* collaborate in each others' fantasies to the point where fantasy becomes the one collective force in the society. The many passages describing the rumors, the expectations, and the reactions of the inhabitants of the town convey the extent to which fantasy has permeated the society:

> The general outburst of hatred with which every one fell upon the "ruffian and dueling bully from the capital" also struck me as curious. They insisted on seeing an insolent design and deliberate intention to insult our whole society at once. [X, 40]

> The impression made on our whole town by the story of the duel, which spread quickly, was particularly remarkable for the unanimity

with which everyone rushed to take Nikolai Vsevolodovich's side. [X, 231]

Two characteristics distinguish Stavrogin from the others who are so concerned with him, and these two characteristics allow him to become the epitome of his society. First, as we have seen, Stavrogin has a special, highly developed fascination for division and contradiction. Second, Stavrogin possesses an unlimited power of self-control, of dissimulation of his emotions, and by virtue of this power he *appears* to others to be indifferent, self-sufficient, a god. But Stavrogin's apparent autonomy is a sham, a mask covering his essential nature. As René Girard has convincingly argued, Stavrogin merely represents the ultimate stage of "metaphysical desire" (what I call fantasy) which possesses the inhabitants of Skvoreshniki.[22]

Stavrogin is the pure distillation of fantasy detached from the grandiose ideas which he has bequeathed to his spiritual progeny. He has passed through the stages of credulity and delusion which his epigones try to recall to his attention and has achieved an awesome lucidity. Yet his own personal fantasy resembles those he has transcended. He has returned to his town in order to announce his marriage to Mar'ja Lebjadkina and to publish his confession as a means of challenging society, of taking off the mask of the cultivated aristocrat and showing the depths of nihilism which he has attained. So Stavrogin in the present is still tempted to carry out a dramatic, resounding act by which he will set himself off from the others and subjugate them with the force of his honesty. Stavrogin apparently views his confession as a publishing event in Russia and abroad. Like Raskol'nikov and Kirillov, he attributes a "world-historical" importance to his act. He tells Tikhon:

"So I decided to have these little sheets printed and to have three hundred copies imported into Russia. When the time comes, I will send them off to the police and the local authorities; simultaneously, I will send them to the editorial offices of all the newspapers with a request for publication and to many of the people who know me in Petersburg and elsewhere in Russia. They will appear uniformly in translation abroad." [XI, 23]

But, although Stavrogin reveals his marriage, he does not publish his confession. His impulse to reveal himself cannot overcome the forces of internalization; he cannot give up his claim to sit in judgment over himself and society. His revelation of himself to Tikhon at the turning point of the plot contains a crucial gap. Stavrogin withholds the second page of his confession, which presumably would clarify the question of whether or not he raped Matresha. But the missing information is not as significant as the act of suppression. At the heart of the novel there is a gaping hole, an affront to the reader's desire to know and a decisive statement of Stavrogin's inability to "think one thing."

Stavrogin's journey has been motivated by his search for an object, a foundation, a connection. In an early plan for the novel in his notebooks, Dostoevsky identifies this quest with that of Russia as a whole. He says of Stavrogin's precursor:

The Prince is seeking a great moral feat, some true accomplishment, something by which Russia would manifest her strength to the whole world. His idea is true, genuine, active Orthodoxy . . . Moral power before economic power.[23]

In the finished novel, this "great moral feat" takes the form of Stavrogin's idea of publishing his confession. In both cases, Dostoevsky emphasizes the protagonist's desire for immediate transformation, but neither the Prince nor Stavrogin can find the means to realize his desire. Neither can mediate between his grandiose ideas and the reality around him. The themes of embodiment, incarnation, and mediation are underscored throughout the notebooks for The Possessed by reference to Christ as an "ideal incarnate" and by repetition of the phrase "Word made flesh."[24] Again in the notebooks, Dostoevsky writes that Tikhon "proves to him [the Prince] that one must not make a leap, but that one must rather regenerate the image of man in oneself (through long-lasting work, and only then vault ahead)."[25] The Prince wants to "start a new breed of men"[26] but he cannot take the first step, as Tikhon says, of achieving self-mastery.[27]

The novel associates Stavrogin's impasse with the lack of a positive inheritance from the past and with the Russian intelligentsia's infatuation with European ideas. There is no generative power in the older generation and nothing to be passed on to the younger generation. Stavrogin's father is absent. We learn that he was a weak, "frivolous old gentleman who died of a stomach disorder on the way to the Crimea, where he was hastening to join the army on active service" (X, 17). He had been separated from Varvara for four years before his death, and until the separation had been supported by her. The brief passage disposing of Stavrogin's father puts him in the same class as Stepan Trofimovich but lacking the latter's cultural aspirations.

Stepan Trofimovich initiates the young Stavrogin into the realm of fantasy.

[He] succeeded in reaching the deepest chords in his friend's heart, and had aroused in him a first vague sensation of that eternal, sacred yearning which some elect souls can never give up for cheap gratification once they have tasted and known it. (There are some connoisseurs who prize this yearning more than the most complete satisfaction of it, if such were possible.) [X, 35]

Presumably, Stepan Trofimovich's infatuation with German idealism and romanticism has led to his estrangement from Russian reality and to his abdication of the role of father. Petr, his son by his first wife, was brought up "in the charge of distant aunts in some remote region" in Russia while Stepan Trofimovich remained in Berlin (X, 11). All Stepan Trofimovich's undertakings are described as aborted. Nothing that he begins is followed through to completion. Here is how the narrator summarizes Stepan Trofimovich's scholarly career:

He only had time to deliver a few lectures, I believe they were about the Arabs; also he defended a brilliant dissertation on the political and Hanseatic importance of the German town Hanau, of which there was promise in the period between 1413 and 1428, and on the special and obscure reasons why that promise was never fulfilled . . . . Later on . . . he published the beginning of a profound investigation into the causes, I believe, of the extraordinary moral nobility of certain knights at a certain period or something of that sort. [X, 8-9]

Stepan Trofimovich's sterility as a scholar, his dependence on Varvara Stavrogina, his pose of "patriotic grief" (X, 12), his imitation of Goethe are all symptoms of his fantastic nature. He is an esthete devoted to a self-indulgent art that ignores reality. He is a liberal Westerner who was so afraid of peasant disturbances following the emancipation "that for some time before the great day he began asking Varvara Petrovna's permission to go abroad" (X, 31). He lives in nostalgia for a past generation which he idealizes—that of the forties, when he had

belonged to a certain distinguished constellation of celebrated leaders of the last generation, when, though only for the briefest moment, his name was pronounced by many hasty persons of that day almost as though it were on a level with the names of Chaadaev, of Belinsky, of Granovsky, and of Herzen . . . . [X, 8]

Stavrogin's search for an object can be seen in the light of Stepan Trofimovich to be the search for a link with the past through a real father. The absence of a substantial father impels Stavrogin on his deepening internal quest. He seeks a ground for his being within himself; he aspires to self-origination. The project of self-origination and the kind of ungrounded thought that Stavrogin pursues are associated by Dostoevsky with Europe. In the notebooks to *The Possessed*, Dostoevsky writes with reference to "the Prince," Stavrogin's predecessor:

it all boils down to one urgent question: can one believe while being civilized, i.e., a European? . . . NB. To this question, civilization gives a factual answer in the negative (Renan) . . . . If this is so, can society exist without faith (on the basis of science alone, for instance)? (Herzen) The moral foundations of a society are given through revelation. Eliminate one thing from religion, and the moral foundation of Christianity will collapse entirely, for everything is mutually linked together.[28]

The progress of European civilization and enlightenment in Russia threatens to destroy Russian faith, and Dostoevsky remarks that "in a hundred years half of Russia will be enlightened."[29] Stavrogin, and through him Dostoevsky, is looking for an answer to the question: "Can one believe at all?"[30] The answer provided by Stavrogin and *The Possessed* as a whole seems overwhelmingly negative. Stavrogin, in his note to Dasha, says that nothing but negation has come from him. He tells her that he looks upon the Russian iconoclasts with spite, from envy of their hopes, but that he could never be one of them (X, 514). In the same note he writes:

"I have tried my strength everywhere . . . . As long as I was experimenting for myself and for others it seemed infinite, as it has all my life. Before your eyes I endured a blow from your brother; I acknowledged my marriage in public. But to what to apply my strength, that is what I've never seen, and do not see now . . . ." [X, 514]

His very formulation of the problem in terms of strength and an object to apply it to reflects the extreme disjunction between himself and the world. He cannot stop experimenting—and experience.

The Possessed dramatizes the threat to both the bonds between individuals of the same generation and those linking one generation with the next. The action of the novel takes place against the initial expectations of a marriage between the unbridled Stavrogin and Liza. The inhabitants of the town see Stavrogin as a threat to society and would like to see him married to Liza. But the expected marriage does not take place, and all other marriages and anticipated marriages in *The Possessed* are aborted. As Edward Said has pointed out, marriages in this novel are unproposed, unconsummated, hidden, or defiled.[31] The news of Stavrogin's marriage to Mar'ja Lebjadkina causes the carnage that follows. Children are

abandoned, commit suicide, or die in infancy. Old men are
helpless and sterile. Kirillov looks forward to the end of proc-
reation. Almost no one survives at the end of *The Possessed*.
The novel seems to call into question the very possibility of
the continuation of human life and society.

The Brothers Karamazov

The Brothers Karamazov takes up again the themes and
problems raised in Dostoevsky's journalistic writings and pursued in the fiction, carrying their implications and intercon-
nections further than any previous work. The drama being
acted out in Skotoprigonevsk has momentous significance for
the future of Russian society. Indeed, Skotoprigonevsk is a
microcosm of Russian society. The conflicts of the Petersburg
period are refracted through the prism of the Karamazov
family and then projected outward for all Russia to see (X,
234, 237).[32] The family, in this novel, more than in any previous novel, becomes the critical unit of society, and its unity
and biological continuity are threatened by the loss of values
which characterizes Petersburg society as a whole. The novel
establishes a correspondence between the most fundamental
biological relations (father-son; brother-brother) and the possibility of human—that is, social—relations in general. In denying his relation to his father, Ivan is denying the possibility
of human relationships, and he is opting for a certain kind of
society.

Fedor Pavlovich's egoism, his individualism, his hoarding
of money and his lust for Grushen'ka threaten the order and
continuity of society. *The Brothers Karamazov* explores
questions raised earlier in *The Diary of a Writer*: What can
present-day fathers pass on to their children? How can sons
escape becoming embittered and resentful and taking their
vengeance on society? In the person of Fedor Pavlovich the
loss of values of the Petersburg period threatens the funda-

mental bonds of human society: paternity, inheritance, genealogy.

In *The Brothers Karamazov* the father, who is absent or weak in the previous novels (*Crime and Punishment, The Idiot*, and *The Possessed*) and mysterious and elusive though central in *A Raw Youth*, becomes central and demystified. The relationship to the father becomes in this novel the model for all other social relations. In bringing the father who denies his sons their inheritance to the fore, Dostoevsky is only bringing into the open the conflict alluded to in *Crime and Punishment*, where the pawnbroker is seen by Raskol'nikov as standing in the way of his career and as denying him his paternal inheritance (his father's watch which he is forced to pawn). Fedor Pavlovich is a true representative of his age: cynical, lacking in self-esteem, and relying on his ability to amass wealth at the expense of the people to whom he sells vodka. The prosecutor characterizes him as "above all a moneylender" (X, 238).[33]

In *The Diary of a Writer* for 1877 Dostoevsky pointed to the importance of the role of fathers in society:

To my way of thinking, the casualness of the contemporary Russian family consists in the loss by modern fathers of every general idea about their families, an idea general to all fathers, tying them all together, which they themselves believe in, and which they would teach their children to believe, conveying to them this faith for their lives.

Please note, this idea, this faith may, perhaps, be erroneous so that the best of children may subsequently renounce it, or, at least, correct it for their own children. Even so, the very existence of such a general idea binding society and the family is already the beginning of order, i.e., moral order, which, naturally, is subject to change, progress, correction, but order just the same. [*Diary*, 759]

... finally, their children matriculate in universities, but there is no father, there is no family; the boy enters life alone because his heart has not lived, *it is not bound with the youth's past, with family or childhood* . . . .

However, this refers only to the rich ones; these are well-off, but are there many who are well-off? The majority, the overwhelming majority are poor. Therefore, in the face of the father's indolence as regards the family, *the children are altogether left to the mercy of chance!* Poverty, the troubles of their fathers are reflected in their hearts in *gloomy pictures, in memories* at times of the most venomous character. Till a very advanced age the children keep recalling their fathers' pusillanimity, quarrels in their families, accusations, bitter reproaches, even curses upon them, for being extra mouths; and what is still worse, sometimes the baseness of their fathers, mean acts perpetrated for the sake of obtaining a position or acquiring money, foul intrigues, hideous servility. And long after, maybe all their lives, the children are inclined blindly to accuse these men, *having derived nothing from their childhood that might mitigate that filth of their memories,* and to size up truthfully, realistically, and, therefore, acquittingly, those years dragged out so sadly. [*Diary*, 761; emphasis added]

This important passage brings together key ideas which underlie *The Brothers Karamazov*: teaching, with its overtones of culture and literacy; faith; a general idea binding fathers and all of society together; and memory as the link between generations. Fedor Pavlovich embodies the loss of a general idea capable of holding society together. He is tormented by his own skepticism and baseness, but he seeks to extend his life as long as possible and to extract maximun pleasure from it. Not believing in immortality or in contact with other worlds, he becomes a miser, jealously hoarding the money which he relies on to prolong his appeal to women. He accumulates money at the expense of others and he poses a threat to young women, whom he lures and exploits. He abandons or "forgets" his children. On the third page of the novel we learn that Fedor Pavlovich "got hold of all her [Adelaida's] money, up to twenty-five thousand rubles, as soon as she received it, so that those thousands were lost to her forever" (X, 13). He then proceeds to forget Mitja, who changes hands five times in the course of his upbringing. After the death of his second wife, Sof'ja, "almost exactly the same thing happened to the two little boys as to the first son Mitja. They were completely forgotten and abandoned by their father" (IX, 20). The theme of abandonment, rejection, denial of relationship is, as we shall see, central to *The Brothers Karamazov*.

Fedor Pavlovich's denial of relationship to his sons more than twenty years previously seems to be what is at issue in the present. Alesha, upon his arrival in Skotoprigonevsk, begins looking for his mother's grave. The narrator says: "Fedor Pavlovich could not show him where his second wife was buried, for he had never visited her grave since he had thrown earth upon her coffin, and in the course of years had entirely forgotten where she was buried" (IX, 30-31). Fedor Pavlovich is said to have gone to Odessa "abandoning the grave and all his memories" (IX, 32). He forgets for a moment that Alesha's mother was also Ivan's mother (IX, 175). The narrator refers to him as "the old profligate who had dropped all family ties" (IX, 121). Fedor Pavlovich denies he is Smerdjakov's father (IX, 127), but he adopts Smerdjakov, who is christened Pavel Fedorovich (IX, 129). He denies any relation to Ivan: "But I don't recognize Ivan, I don't know him at all. Where does he come from? His soul is completely different from ours" (IX, 219). He curses Mitja and offers Alesha his blessing only to change his mind. Fedor Pavlovich's denial of his relationship to his sons culminates in his rejection of the idea of leaving a will and his admission that he wants all his money for himself (IX, 219).

Each of the four brothers reacts differently to his rejection, to his denial of a spiritual inheritance. Mitja submits to the Karamazov bug and is driven by his sensuality. Alesha retains the memory of his mother and adopts Zosima as his spiritual father. Smerdjakov consciously hides his hatred of Fedor Pavlovich and the three legitimate sons while cursing his lot and seeking revenge. Smerdjakov reveals the cause of his resentment when he says: "I am descended from a filthy beggar and have no father" (IX, 281). Ivan's relationship with his father is the most obscure. The narrator cannot find a satisfactory explanation for Ivan's visit, "which was the first step leading to so many consequences."

It seemed strange on the face of it that a young man so learned, so proud, and apparently so cautious, should suddenly visit such an infamous house and a father who had ignored him all his life, hardly knew him, never thought of him, and would not under any circumstances have given him money, though he was always afraid that his sons Ivan and Alexei would also come one day to ask him for it. And here the young man was staying in the house of such a father, had been living with him for two months, and they were on the best possible terms. [IX, 24]

If we can believe Smerdjakov, Ivan is more like Fedor Pavlovich than any of the latter's other sons (X, 157). There is a deep kinship between Fedor Pavlovich, Ivan, and Smerdjakov; and these two sons resemble their father and are closer to him spiritually than Mitja, who wrestles openly with his Karamazov nature.

What unites them is their denial of relations and their impulse to conceal, dissemble, and hoard. It is impossible to tell whether Fedor Pavlovich is joking or not, whether he believes his lies or not. Smerdjakov's argumentation in "The Controversy" has the same detached, ironical character as Fedor Pavlovich's stories, and so does Ivan's article on the ecclesiastic courts. Smerdjakov and Ivan are withdrawn and resentful, like Fedor Pavlovich, and they both, in almost identical words, deny any relation to Mitja, whom they despise. Smerdjakov says to Alesha: "How am I to know about Dmitrii Fedorovich? It's not as if I were his keeper" (IX, 284). Six pages later, Ivan asks Alesha: "What have I to do with it? Am I my brother Dmitrii's keeper?" (IX, 290). Ivan wants to wash his hands of his entanglements in Skotoprigonevsk and to go to Europe (IX, 289). Smerdjakov hates his position and says he would have left long ago if he only had money (IX, 283). He dreams of going to France. They both want to break with the present and at the same time to take revenge for their sufferings. They are both distracted, like Fedor Pavlovich, by some thought which intrudes into their consciousness. They are both in the grip of fantasy. Smerdjakov's peculiar state of mind is described in terms which link him to both Ivan and Fedor Pavlovich:

If it had occurred to any one to wonder at the time what the young man was interested in, and what was in his mind, it would have been impossible to tell by looking at him. Yet sometimes he would stop suddenly in the house, or even in the yard or street, and would stand still for ten minutes, lost in thought . . . . Yet probably he has, hidden within himself, the impression which had dominated him during the period of contemplation. Those impressions are dear to him and no doubt he hoards them imperceptibly, and even unconsciously . . . . [IX, 161]

Ivan withdraws into himself and elaborates his arguments against the world as it is. He draws up an indictment against God's creation based on the suffering of innocent children. Ivan, the intellectual and socialist, elaborates his blueprint for utopia, a society in which the child-like masses will be shielded by guardians who will take upon themselves the burden of suffering and uncertainty.

It is in the chapter "Rebellion" that Ivan draws up his indictment which is directed, by implication, at a religion and a society which justify suffering as a necessary concomitant of human freedom. Ivan recounts five stories which he has taken from newspapers. The first is about the Turks' torture of Slav children in Bulgaria; the second is the story of Richard and his trial in Switzerland; and the last three involve the torture of Russian children by their parents and the mutilation of a serf-child at the command of his master. What is the significance of these stories, aside from revealing Ivan's morbidity and providing a rationale for his rejection of the world? Are we, in other words, to take these stories at face value, as objective, "Euclidean" facts as Ivan offers them, or do they reveal something essential about Ivan's unconscious preoccupations? Both the content and the order of the stories suggest that Ivan has something specific in mind.

After the first anecdote, he says: "The Turks, of course, have been included in it [his collection of atrocity stories], but they are foreigners. I have specimens from home that are even better than the Turks" (IX, 300). He then goes on to distinguish the Turks from Europeans and includes the Russians among Europeans. He proceeds to distinguish Russians from Europeans in their methods of punishment though he qualifies this distinction. And as an example of European hypocrisy and philanthropy, he tells the story of Richard, the illegitimate child who was neglected and treated like an animal by his foster parents and who ended by being condemned to death for murdering and robbing an old man (IX, 300). Ivan then goes on to speak of the Russian peasant's cruelty to animals, and the remaining three anecdotes emphasize the refinement of cruelty among "well-educated, cultured" Russians (IX, 302, 303, 304). The progression of the five anecdotes thus leads ever closer to home. It appears, after all, that Ivan's preoccupation with the torture of children is not disinterested. If we conflate the stories we see that Ivan is talking about children who are abandoned or neglected and then punished (by society/angry parents/master) for committing a "crime" (robbery and murder/not asking to be taken to the privy/accidently injuring the dog's paw). It should be clear from this that Ivan is referring to his own (and his brothers') treatment by Fedor Pavlovich. He says that Richard grew up "like a little beast. The shepherds taught him nothing, and scarcely fed or clothed him, but sent him out at seven to herd the flock in cold and wet, and no one hesitated or scrupled to treat him so" (IX, 300). The fact that Richard is illegitimate and that the victim of the fifth anecdote is a serf link Ivan's resentment against his father with Smerdjakov, the most extreme case of rejection. Finally, in the last anecdote, the mention of "dependents and buffoons" (IX, 304) brings Fedor Pavlovich to mind. "Dependent" (*prizhival'shchik*) and "buffoon" (*shut*) are two of the most common characterizations of Fedor Pavlovich (IX, 11, 13, 51; X, 238).

Ivan thus reveals his motivation in "confining ourselves to the sufferings of children . . . though it does weaken my case" (IX, 298). What he formulates as a general, global indictment of creation has its origin in his personal history. Ivan's project of shaking society to its foundations, of radical transformation by his denial of immortality and his assertion that "everything is permitted," has for its foundation a tortured child, and that child is Ivan Karamazov. We must now turn to Ivan's Grand Inquisitor in order to see how Ivan's view of history and society reflect his relation to his father.

In a letter to Ljubimov from May 10, 1879, Dostoevsky refers to the fifth book of *The Brothers Karamazov* as "the culminating point of the novel" (*Pis'ma*, IV, 53). Several months later, in a letter to Konstantin Pobedonostsev, he expresses his doubts about being able to present an effective rebuttal to Ivan's ideas:

As for the answer to this whole *negative side*, I had planned this sixth book, "A Russian Monk," which will appear on August 31st. I am trembling over it: Will it be an adequate answer, especially since it is not a direct answer to the position expressed (in the G. Inquisitor and preceding it) point by point, but only an oblique one? This is directly contrary to the world view expressed earlier, but again it is not presented point by point but, so to speak, in an artistic picture. This is what disturbs me: Will I be understood, and will I attain my goal at all? [*Pis'ma*, IV, 109; emphasis in original]

Dostoevsky here expresses his concern with the polemical thrust of the two books which state the opposed positions of Ivan and Zosima. He speaks of "The Grand Inquisitor" chapter as if it were a set piece rather than part of the fabric of a complex novel. Specifically, there is no awareness that "The Grand Inquisitor" is not just a statement of a political-moral position. It is also part of the characterization of Ivan Karamazov and, when seen in the context of the novel, it contains its own refutation. In Ivan Karamazov and "The Grand Inquisitor," Dostoevsky brings together his judgments about socialism and Western civilization as they had evolved over the previous twenty years[34] with his insight into how certain ideas are held by individuals. In my concluding chapter, I will argue that in his later fiction, Dostoevsky makes use of ideas which he had already explored in his journalistic writings and that his creative movement is "from ideology to imagination" or from ideas strongly held to a consideration of the origin of these ideas and the ways in which they are held. For now, I want to propose an explanation of how "The Grand Inquisitor" may be integrated into the surrounding text of the the the novel and how it is to be seen as "the culminating point of the novel" not just ideologically, but imaginatively. There is no question that Dostoevsky regarded "The Grand Inquisitor" as a distillation of his criticism of socialism and atheism, but at the same time, as a novelist he went further than in any previous novel in anchoring beliefs and actions in character. Interpretations of "The Grand Inquisitor" have tended to treat it as an expendable digression, as an expression of existential truths about the human condition, or as Dostoevsky's exposition of the logic of Catholicism and socialism.[35] I hope to show that "The Grand Inquisitor" is intimately connected with the rest of the novel and that it serves the purposes of fiction as well as, if not better than, those of polemic.

The "Grand Inquisitor" chapter follows Ivan's catalogue of tortures in the chapter "Rebellion." After presenting his indictment of the world, Ivan proceeds to his vision of a utopia in which the suffering of the majority will be abolished. But something has changed between the two chapters. While Ivan takes the part of the tortured children and refuses any future harmony in their name, the Grand Inquisitor, in spite of his love for humanity, looks with contempt on the childish and weak suffering masses. Suffering, which in "Rebellion" was associated with innocent children, is in "The Grand Inquisitor" associated with the rulers who have taken the "terrible burden of freedom" upon themselves in order to provide happiness for the rest of mankind. Suffering becomes a mark of distinction for the elite. In the course of dividing society into a majority of ordinary, weak people and a minority who can bear suffering, the Grand Inquisitor has come to despise the masses. Ivan's judgment of human nature provides the basis for his utopia.

The Grand Inquisitor accuses Christ of having shown insensitivity to mankind's suffering by placing freedom of conscience above material welfare. He argues that only the powers of miracle, mystery, and authority can secure man's happiness and solve the problem of his social organization. By accepting miracle, mystery, and authority, Christ, the Grand Inquisitor says, would have "accomplished all that man seeks on earth—that is, someone to worship, someone to keep his conscience, and some means of uniting all in one unanimous and harmonious ant-heap" (IX, 323-24). The Grand Inquisitor has taken the side of the devil in order to complete the tower of Babel, the erection of a self-sufficient human society without God. In this society the masses will be shielded from the tormenting knowledge of good and evil and will be deceived with the promise of a nonexistent afterlife. Only a hundred thousand rulers will have to endure the terrible truth in order to maintain a static, contented society in its state of childlike ignorance. The Grand Inquisitor puts into practice Mitja's idea of narrowing man. He would create the "one flock" that Dostoevsky refers to in the "Baal" chapter of *Winter Notes*.[36]

The Grand Inquisitor's equation of the masses with children indicates the shift that has taken place in Ivan's attitude from the previous chapter. The contempt and hatred that in "Rebellion" were focused on those in authority are in "The Grand Inquisitor" focused on the weak, vile suffering masses. The following passages from the Grand Inquisitor's monologue show the insistence on this point:

"They will be convinced, too, that they can never be free, for they are weak, vicious, worthless and rebellious." [IX, 318]

"But Thou didst think too highly of men therein, for they are slaves, of course, though they are rebellious by nature." [IX, 321]

"He [man] is weak and vile. What though he is everywhere now rebelling against our power, and proud of his rebellion? It is the pride of a child and a schoolboy. They are little children rioting and barring out the teacher from the school. But their childish delight will come to an end and it will cost them dear. They will cast down temples and drench the earth with blood. But they will see at last, the foolish children, that, though they are rebels, they are impotent rebels, unable to keep up their own rebellion. Bathed in their foolish tears, they will recognize at last that He who has created them rebels must have meant to mock them." [IX, 322]

"Then we shall give them the quiet humble happiness of weak creatures such as they are by nature."[IX, 325]

"We shall show them that they are weak, that they are only pitiful children, but that childlike happiness is the sweetest of all . . . . They will marvel at us and will be awe-striken before us and will be proud at our being so powerful and clever, that we have been able to subdue such a turbulent flock of thousands of millions. They will tremble impotently before our wrath, their minds will grow fearful, they will be quick to shed tears like women and children . . . ." [IX, 325]

"and they will adore us as their saviors who have taken on themselves their sins before God." [IX, 326]

"Though if there were anything in the other world, it certainly would not be for such as they." [IX, 326]

To the extent that the Grand Inquisitor expresses Ivan's solution to an intolerable world, Ivan has stepped into the role of the Father who despises his children. Ivan the Europeanized intellectual and student of natural science takes over from Ivan the Russian schoolboy of the "Rebellion" chapter. In order to transform the world, the helpless child must become an all-powerful father ("they will adore us as their saviors"). But Ivan (in his Grand Inquisitor) betrays his infantile attachment by the high price he puts on suffering.

Ivan reveals himself when he sardonically interprets Katerina Ivanovna's decision to remain faithful to Dmitrii. Ivan describes Katerina Ivanovna, in the same terms as the

Grand Inquisitor, as wanting to sacrifice herself in order to exalt herself:

"in anyone else this moment would be only due to yesterday's impression and would be only a moment. But with Katerina Ivanovna's character, that moment will last all her life . . . a painful brooding over your own feelings, your own heroism, and your own suffering; but in the end that suffering will be softened and will pass into sweet contemplation of the fulfillment of a bold and proud design."[IX, 238]

Ivan, too, is attached to the cause of his suffering but is not consciously aware of it:

"I am a bug, and I recognize in all humility that I cannot understand why the world is arranged as it is. Men are themselves to blame, I suppose; they were given paradise, they wanted freedom, and stole fire from heaven, though they knew they would become unhappy, so there is no reason to pity them. With my pitiful, earthly, Euclidean understanding, all I know is that there is suffering and that there are none guilty; that cause follows effect, simply and directly . . . . What comfort is it to me that there are none guilty and that cause follows effect simply and directly, and that I know it—I must have retribution, or I will destroy myself."[IX, 305-06]

The injustice of the torture of children is compounded by Ivan's awareness of his own potential for evil conveyed by Liza's allusions to her conversations with Ivan. Ivan, too, has inherited the Karamazov nature, which he attempts to suppress, to overcome in himself. What accounts for Ivan's fascination-repulsion toward his father is his similarity to Fedor Pavlovich. This is the great injustice, that he, Ivan Karamazov, could be capable of the same cruel, base impulses, that he could be so much like his father. And this is what he has to justify to himself and "correct" in his poem about "The Grand Inquisitor." But the contradictions remain and are carried over into his theory: "all is permitted," yet he would set up a despotism in which the elite acts as the conscience and the warders of the weak masses. His intellectualizing bears the imprint of his psychic conflict: he wants to do away with his own father and with God the Father and proclaim his own freedom as a man-god, but he merely steps into the role of the oppressive father. This is the unconscious conflict that Smerdjakov and the devil bring out into the light of consciousness.

Ivan's main trait seems to be self-control. Mitja expresses his anger openly and violently, and Ivan seems to despise him for it. Ivan's anger, on the other hand, escapes him only momentarily, as when he brutally knocks Maksimov off the moving carriage, or when he asks his father whether Alesha's mother was not his mother too (IX, 175). Ivan assures Alesha that he would defend his father against Mitja but that he reserves "full latitude" in his wishes (IX, 182). It is in his writings (dealing with the organization of society) that Ivan gives indirect expression to his revulsion with his father, and these can only be understood as reactions against the reality that his father represents to him. Ivan's whole set of beliefs, it would seem, has been adopted as a reaction against his father.

The extent of Ivan's internalization of his father's image is conveyed by the shape his devil takes and by the tone and tendency of the devil's remarks. Ivan's devil bears a striking resemblance to Fedor Pavlovich.[37] Ivan's attempt to deny his relation to his father and to assert his total independence, his project of self-origination, is exposed in its true light by his hallucination of the devil.

Both Fedor Pavlovich and the devil are described as having been in a dependent position (*prizhival'shchiki*) (IX, 3, 11; X, 161, 238). They are both garrulous and ingratiating. They both tell stories about philosophers. They both quote French and refer to French philosophy: Fedor Pavlovich refers to Diderot and Voltaire; the devil alludes to Descartes. They both refer to writers and to works of literature: Fedor Pavlovich to de Sade, to *A Hero of Our Time*, to *Die Räuber*, and the devil to Tolstoy, Belinsky, Heine, *Dead Souls*, and *Faust*. They both criticize lofty ideals and romanticism, and express their faith in earthbound "realism." They both lack faith but long for it. They both imply that religious men are hypocrites and sensualists: Fedor Pavlovich's ramblings about the monks at monasteries and the devil's story about the Jesuit priest who seduces the young girl who confesses to him. Fedor Pavlovich calls Zosima a Jesuit (IX, 172). Both claim to be maligned, Fedor Pavlovich for his degrading buffoonery and the devil for providing the necessary minus sign in the scheme of creation. They are both superstitious, squeamish, and inclined to hypochondria. The devil's "if only there could be an ax there" (X, 167) echoes Fedor Pavlovich's puzzling over how there could be a hell without hooks (IX, 34). They both extol pleasure and sin. They are both mocking and irreverent. The devil's "*Satan sum et nihil humanum a me alienum puto*"[38] evokes Fedor Pavlovich's declaration that he is the "father of lies" (IX, 59) and his thirst for life, his desire to experience everything, to love every woman.

The description of the devil's background would seem to clinch the association with Fedor Pavlovich:

Such hangers-on, gentlemen of accommodating temper, who can tell a story, take a hand at cards, and who have a distinct aversion for any duties that may be forced upon them are usually solitary creatures, either bachelors or widowers. Sometimes they have children, but if so the children are always being brought up somewhere far away, at some aunts', to whom these gentlemen never allude in good society, seeming ashamed of the relationship. They gradually lose sight of their children altogether . . . . [X, 161]

Ivan's attempt to deny his own history (family history) dooms him to internalize it. Smerdjakov, who says that Ivan is more like his father than any of the other sons, sees deeply into Ivan beneath Ivan's civility and culture to his identification with his father.

The three interviews with Smerdjakov lead up to the appearance of Ivan's devil. Smerdjakov, by virtue of his access to the unconscious, acquires power over his master Ivan. With each interview, Smerdjakov tightens the chain linking Ivan to his father's murder. In the three meetings over a period of two months they subject their conversation at the gate the night before the murder to scrupulous exegesis, and Smerdjakov leads Ivan relentlessly to the real significance of their exchange. In the first interview, Smerdjakov claims that he was trying to persuade Ivan to stay by telling him to go to Chermashnja rather than Moscow. He claims he was trying to convey his apprehension that something would happen and that he wanted Ivan to be near. Ivan feels relieved after the first interview by Smerdjakov's assurance that it was not himself but Dmitrii who committed the murder (X, 128). But there is something in Smerdjakov's parting promise not to refer to their conversation at the gate which disturbs him, and "he felt as though he wanted to make haste to forget something" (X, 128). The memory of his creeping out onto the stairs to listen on his last night in his father's house returns to him, and he goes to see Smerdjakov a second time. This time Smerdjakov comes out and says that Ivan wished his father's death, and Ivan strikes him. Smerdjakov now interprets Ivan's last-minute acquiescence in going to Chermashnja as compliance in his father's murder (X, 136). When Ivan repeats the conversation to Katerina Ivanovna, she shows him Mitja's letter in order to convince Ivan of Mitja's guilt. After a month, however, Katerina reveals that she is not at all sure of Mitja's guilt, and Ivan goes to see Smerdjakov a third time. This time Smerdjakov makes no effort to disguise his contempt and anger at Ivan. When Ivan demands to be told everything, Smerdjakov says: "Well, it was you who murdered him." "*You* murdered him; you are the real murderer, I was only your instrument, your faithful servant, and it was following your words I did it" (X, 144–45). But Smerdjakov realizes that Ivan is not conscious of his role in the murder and undertakes to explain the whole sequence of events to him:

"But I don't want to lie to you now, because— because if you really haven't understood anything so far—and I see you haven't—and are not just pretending so as to foist the blame on to me to my very face, you are still responsible for everything, since you knew about the murder and charged me to do it, and went away knowing all about it. And so I want to prove to your face this evening that you are the principal murderer in this whole affair, and that I am not the principal murderer, though I did commit the murder. You are the real murderer." [X, 149–50]

It is Smerdjakov, the valet, who assumes power through his position as outcast. His rejection by Fedor and by Grigorii is more extreme than that of the other three sons. He is an outcast among outcasts. His name, which means "the stinker," marks him off from the rest of society and reminds him of his birth. Grigorii calls him a "monster" and asks if he is human (IX, 158). Fedor Pavlovich calls him Balaam's ass (IX, 158). Grigorii's slapping Smerdjakov when he is twelve years old is apparently the cause of his epilepsy (IX, 158). Ivan, whom Smerdjakov admires, looks on him with disdain: "he's a lackey and a mean soul. Raw material, however, when the time comes" (IX, 168). During Ivan's second interview with Smerdjakov, Ivan calls him a "stinking rogue" and hits him (X, 133–34).

Smerdjakov, by virtue of his detachment, his radical exclusion from society, asserts his belonging to the community of the unconscious. He asserts a connection between Ivan and himself and between Ivan and Fedor Pavlovich. In the third interview, he mocks Ivan's determination to testify against himself at the trial with the following words:

"It isn't possible. You are very clever. I know you like money and you also like to be respected because you are very proud. You are excessively fond of female charms, and, most of all, you like living in undisturbed comfort without having to bow to anyone—that's what you care most about. You won't want to spoil your life forever by taking such a disgrace on yourself in court. You are like Fedor Pavlovich; you are the most like him of all his children; you have the same soul he had."[X, 157]

Smerdjakov, who has been denied any inheritance and who resents his lack of a father (IX, 281), ascribes to Ivan a desire for the money he would inherit upon Fedor Pavlovich's death. By killing Fedor Pavlovich he had hoped that Ivan, his mentor, would have "rewarded me when you were able, all the rest of your life" (X, 150). He is disappointed in Ivan, as Svidrigailov is in Raskol'nikov. Since Smerdjakov and Svidrigailov are both creatures of fantasy and resentment, they fail to see the fantastic elements in the projects of their adopted heroes. Both Smerdjakov and Svidrigailov have no means of escape but suicide. Ivan's project of becoming a man-god, of transgressing, of providing a new model and a new law for mankind that would transform society fails, as do Raskol'nikov's and Stavrogin's.

The denial of relationship is carried to great lengths in *The Brothers Karamazov*. Throughout the novel people continually deny that they are related by kinship or that they resemble one another. Miusov denies he is related to Fedor Pavlovich. Rakitin denies he is related to Grushen'ka. Fedor Pavlovich's abandonment of his children is a denial of his relation to them. In addition, he curses his son Mitja. He denies that Smerdjakov is related to him. He cannot "recognize" Ivan. Ivan says that he is not responsible for Mitja. Smerjakov says he is not responsible for Mitja. Ivan says he has nothing to do with Smerdjakov.

The novel sets up an analogy between the denial of relationship by individuals and society's denial of relationship to the criminal. Here Dostoevsky returns to the issue of the criminal and his relation to a punishing society which he first broached in *Notes from the House of the Dead*. Ivan treats this question in his article on the ecclesiastic courts which Father Paisii summarizes. In this article Ivan puts forward a different version of utopia from that contained in his "Grand Inquisitor" (although Miusov confuses the two) (IX, 87). He argues that in the present in Russia the state exercises the right of punishment while the Russian Church looks upon the convicted criminal with pity: "the Church, like a tender, loving mother, holds aloof from active punishment herself, as the sinner is too severely punished already by the civil law"

(IX, 84). The Church in Russia provides a counterweight to civil punishment and "always keeps up relations with the criminal as a dear and precious son" (IX, 85). Ivan raises the possibility that in the future the state will be absorbed by the Church, and Zosima envisages a time when the Church's moral judgment would coincide with the judgment of the society as a whole:

"the Church's judgment would have an influence on the reformation of the criminal which it does not have at present . . . . and the Church would understand the criminal and the crime of the future in many ways quite differently than now and would be able to restore the excluded, restrain those who plan evil, and regenerate the fallen." [IX, 85]

Russian society of the present, where the Church occupies only a secondary role, and European society, where the Church is moribund, reject and abandon the criminal, with whom they wish to deny any relation:

"all these sentences to exile with hard labor, and formerly with flogging also, reform no one, and what's more, deter hardly a single criminal, and the number of crimes does not diminish but is continually on the increase. You must admit that. Consequently, the security of society is not preserved, for, although the obnoxious member is mechanically cut off and sent far away out of sight, another criminal always comes to take his place at once, and often two of them." [IX, 83]

"The foreign criminal, they say, rarely repents, for the very doctrines of today confirm him in the idea that his crime is not a crime but only a reaction against an unjustly oppressive force. Society cuts him off completely by a force that triumphs over him mechanically and . . . accompanies this exclusion with hatred, forgetfulness, and the most profound indifference as to the ultimate fate of the erring brother." [IX, 84-85]

The story of Richard and the story of Mitja exemplify the reaction of European society and Europeanized Russian society to the criminal. In telling the story of Richard, Ivan implies that the philanthropic and missionary zeal of Genevan society represents a ritualized denial of any deep respon-

sibility for Richard's ordeal. By executing Richard, the Gene-
vans mask their own guilt, holding him mechanically
responsible for his crime. The story of Richard anticipates the
judgment passed on Mitja by Skotoprigonevsk society.

The trial and the judgment that the court passes on Mitja are a judgment of Russian society's ability to perceive the
truth—and they prove to be a withering judgment. The murder takes place almost precisely in the center of the novel,
and the attempt to arrive at the truth of who killed Fedor
Pavlovich occupies most of the latter half, with the preliminary investigation, Ivan's interviews with Smerdjakov, and the
trial which takes up 100 pages. But as the novel progresses
from the last interview with Smerdjakov to the trial, the truth
becomes increasingly distorted in the welter of biased, self-
serving, rhetorical interpretations. The truth which Smerdjakov conveys to Ivan in their last interview cannot be made
public, cannot be assimilated by the larger society. After
Smerdjakov's suicide, it remains trapped inside Ivan, who
sinks into brain fever.

The attitude of the citizens of Skotoprigonevsk toward
Mitja reveals their limited capacity for perceiving truth:

A peculiar fact—established afterwards by many observations—was
that almost all the ladies, or at least a majority of them, were on
Mitja's side and in favor of his being acquitted. [X, 188]

In fact, one may say pretty certainly that the masculine, as distinguished from the feminine part of the audience was biased against
the prisoner. [X, 189]

Everyone, perhaps, felt from the first that the case was beyond
dispute, that there was no doubt about it, that there could really be
no discussion, and that the defense was only a matter of form, and
that the prisoner was guilty, obviously and conclusively guilty. I
imagine that even the ladies, who were so impatiently longing for
the acquittal of the interesting prisoner, were at the same time,
without exception, convinced of his guilt. [X, 195-96]

The women pride themselves on their liberalism and humani-
tarianism—but it is clear that they find the reckless and turbu-

lent Dmitrii attractive. The men are motivated by jealousy of Dmitrii and the desire to see his unrestrained conduct punished. But the two groups are equally convinced of his guilt and enjoy the drama of the trial.

Liza recognizes the duplicity of the town's reaction:

"You know, it's as though people have made an agreement to lie about it and have lied about it ever since. They all declare that they hate evil, but secretly they all love it . . . . Listen, your brother is being tried now for murdering his father and everyone loves his having killed his father . . . . Yes, loves it, everyone loves it. Everybody says it's so awful, but secretly they simply love it. I for one love it." (X, 94)

And Ivan calls the trial by its proper name when he says: "It's a spectacle they want. Bread and circuses!" (X, 226).

After having been led to the truth of his own repressed impulses by Smerdjakov, Ivan perceives a truth about society and civil law which amplifies and deepens the insight contained in the story of Richard. Richard had robbed and killed "an old man" after having been abandoned and treated like an animal. Mitja is accused of having robbed and murdered his "old man" after having been abandoned and neglected. The outcast, who always poses a threat to the security of society, is hated and feared by those who reject him. Dmitrii is found guilty of the murder of his father because he acted the part, because he threatened a society based on decorum, rejection, denial of relationship, and repression. This is the truth that Ivan blurts out in court:

"Who doesn't desire his father's death? . . . My father has been murdered and they pretend they are horrified . . . . They keep up the sham with one another. Liars! They all desire the death of their fathers." [X, 225]

Dmitrii is made a scapegoat not because his behavior is foreign to the society but because every member of it senses in himself the impulses which Dmitrii fails to restrain. Dmitrii is convicted for his lack of decorum, for his lack of repression, for his uncontainable energy and passion, for his breadth which society cannot tolerate.

As Freud put it in *Totem and Taboo*:

In order to keep the temptation down, the envied transgressor must be deprived of the fruit of his enterprise; and the punishment will not infrequently give those who carry it out an opportunity of committing the same outrage under colour of an act of expiation. This is indeed one of the foundations of the human penal system and it is based, no doubt correctly, on the assumption that the prohibited impulses are present alike in the criminal and in the avenging community.[39]

Thus, the trial makes clear that the final denial of relationship belongs to society. It is only through the narrative of these denials of relationship and the fantasy on which they are based that a deeper image of society can be affirmed. Zosima with his vision of the interconnectedness of all things and of personal responsibility for everyone articulates the truth which the fiction approaches through the failed attempts at mediation. Zosima says that we are all guilty—those who seclude themselves from the world and temptation more than others—and thus each is responsible for all. "Until you have become really, in actual fact, a brother to everyone, brotherhood will not come to pass" (X, 379–80).

6

CREATIVE PROCESS: FROM IDEOLOGY TO IMAGINATION

But it was precisely the fortuitous, unavoidable way in which I had come upon the sensation that guaranteed the truth of a past which that sensation revived and of the mental images it released, since we feel its effort to come up into the light and also the thrill of recapturing reality. . . . No matter what idea life may have implanted within us, its material representation, the outline of the impression it has made upon us, is always the guarantee of its indispensable truth.

—Proust, *Remembrance of Things Past*, II, 1001

ALL OF Dostoevsky's writings after 1860 have a common preoccupation: to point to the resolution of certain vexing contradictions in Russian reality—above all, the gulf between the people and the intelligentsia and Russia's problematic relation to Europe. In this regard, there is undoubtedly a basic unity between Dostoevsky's journalism and his fiction, and it makes sense to use the former to shed light on the latter, as many critics and biographers of Dostoevsky have done. At the same time, the sensibilities underlying the journalism and the fiction are radically opposed. Most readers have been disturbed by the xenophobia, anti-Semitism, Great Russian chauvinism, and strident messianism which Dostoevsky gives vent to in *The Diary*, and critics have frequently invoked the distinction between the propagandist and the artist to demarcate the two conflicting sensibilities.[1] Few, if any, however, have pursued this contradiction to the point of asking: how could the same person who wrote *The Brothers Karamazov* have written, with unquestionable sincerity, certain passages in *The Diary of a Writer*? This question should take us beyond the neat distinction between the artist and the propagandist—suggesting as it does masks which can be taken off and put on in different situations—and lead us to see two disparate facets of Dostoevsky's personality as being vitally interrelated.

In a general way, Dostoevsky's two large bodies of work, his journalism and his fiction, can be characterized by two distinct styles of thought which I call the ideological and the imaginative modes. Ideology, in the sense in which I am using it here, represents a relation to the world based on rigid boundaries and rejection (one could even say excommunication) of all that appears alien and problematic. Imagination represents a higher order of relationship, more comprehensive, more open, and based on mediation between apparent contraries: self-other, appearance-essence. It is my assumption that these two styles of thought, in turn, reflect fundamental psychological attitudes in Dostoevsky. If this is so, one can ask: what is the function of these two attitudes in Dostoevsky's mental economy and what is the relation between them? In this chapter, I will first try to characterize Dostoevsky's ideologizing and suggest its psychological function. Then I will discuss two instances in which Dostoevsky starts out in the ideological mode and, after exhausting its possibilities, achieves a state of integration in which new truths are revealed to him. The dramatic shift in perspective which Dostoevsky describes in these two cases sheds light on his creative process. Ideology, and the emotions which underlie it, seems to constitute an initial and psychologically primitive response to a contradiction, to frustration. Dostoevsky arrives at a level of integration, acceptance, and artistic vision, not immediately but only after freeing himself from his ideological impulse. Ideology is thus both an obstacle and a stepping-stone to imagination.

Throughout *The Diary* one feels Dostoevsky's pronouncements and the solutions he advocates to be at odds with his copious and compelling description of the problems facing post-reform Russia. At the very least, one feels his "solutions" to be abstract, willful, and arbitrary, imposed upon the material rather than flowing from it. There is a discrepancy between Dostoevsky's probing examination of the dilemmas of Russian society and the statements of belief and exhortations which he offers as solutions. In the latter passages, Dostoevsky is the very opposite of what his narrators are in the fiction: playful, detached, entertaining opposing points of view with the same fullness.[2] In the ideological passages in *The Diary* his voice is authoritarian, dogmatic, petulant—a voice validating itself by assertion alone, a voice not subject to self-questioning, to the playful rebuttal that we find in, say, the narrator of *Notes from Underground*.

The imaginative mode allows free play in the exploration of important phenomena; it is relativistic, non-authoritarian, and self-critical. It exposes "absolute" differences between self and other as the product of repression and is free to discover hidden relations between seemingly unrelated terms.[3] The imaginative mode allows Dostoevsky to explore certain ideas and regions without having either to take responsibility for his characters or to divorce himself from them, and without having to assert his own beliefs directly.[4]

If the imaginative mode entails the calling into question of accepted categories and the dissolution (or relaxation) of boundaries, the ideological mode gives expression to a concern for the maintenance of distinct boundaries. Dostoevsky's ideologizing appears to function as a defense against a personal anxiety bound up with the problem of Russia's historical identity. It has all the hallmarks of an emotionally invested "system." Dostoevsky the ideologist is authoritarian and resorts to assertions about the future based only on belief. He emphasizes differences rather than exploring their origins and the means of overcoming them. His assertions are abstract and absolute, making continual reference to "the people," "Orthodoxy," and "Russia's historic mission." Two passages in *The Diary* reveal Dostoevsky's ideologizing in its starkest terms.

In *The Diary* for September 1876, Dostoevsky takes issue with an article on the so-called "Eastern question" (the oppression of Slavs within the Turkish empire). The author of this article had criticized the religious tone of the Russian movement in support of the Slavs for being offensive to the Muslim minority within the Russian empire. Dostoevsky characterizes the author of the article (whom he does not name) as an antiquated representative of Russian Europeanism of the Granovsky type, one of the "last of the Mohicans" who are out of touch with the people and have no understanding of Russian reality (*Diary*, pp. 442ff.).[5] Dostoevsky, who views the popular enthusiasm for the uprisings of the Slavs against the Turkish empire as a sign of Russia's awakening national consciousness, attacks his opponent and ascribes responsibility for the religious tone of the conflict to the Mohammedans: ". . . I venture to assert that in the view of any Mohammedan, help given to a Gentile against a Mohammedan, no matter under what pretext, is absolutely equivalent to help given to a Gentile on the grounds of religion" (*Diary*, p. 448). Up to this point Dostoevsky's arguments seem rational if unenlightened. He goes on, however, to justify his position by appealing to the way France would surely deal with agitation among her Muslim subjects during a hypothetical war between France and Turkey (*Diary*, p. 449). The incongruity of Dostoevsky's citing the practice of a European government (and the one he despises most) as justification for Russia's attitude toward its Muslim minority should alert us that he is on shaky ground. In any event, he proceeds to an outburst against the Tartars which begs attention for its ferocity:

The Russian land belongs to the Russian, to the Russians *alone*; it is Russian land, and in it *there isn't an inch of Tartar land*. The Tartars are the former tormentors of the Russian land; they are aliens in this land. But the Russians, having subdued the Tartars, having recaptured from them their land and having conquered them, did not punish the Tartars for the tortures of two centuries; they have not humiliated them in the the manner in which the Muslim Turks have humbled the Gentiles who have never offended them; on the contrary, the Russians have granted the Tartars such full civic equality as, perhaps, you will not find in the most civilized countries in the West which, according to you, is so enlightened. Perhaps the Mohammedan, at times, has even abused his high privileges, to the detriment of the Russian—the owner and master of the Russian land. . . . Nor did the Russians humble the Tartars' religion; they have neither persecuted nor oppressed them. Believe me, nowhere in the West, nowhere in the whole world, will you find such a broad, such a humane, religious tolerance as in the soul of a real Russian. Believe me also that it is rather the Tartar who is inclined to shun the Russian (precisely because of the former's Mohammedanism) than vice versa. This will be corroborated by anyone who has lived among the Tartars. Nevertheless, the master of the Russian land is the Russian (Great Russian, Little Russian, White Russian—they are all the same). Thus it shall always be. [*Diary*, pp. 449-50; emphasis in original]

Here, all pretense to rational argument breaks down and Dostoevsky falls back on a series of vehement and bald assertions, devoid of all reference to particulars or personal experience. We are told nothing of this Tartar, his history, his relation to Russian society, nothing except the mention of the Tartar yoke, which ended in 1480. Dostoevsky asserts that even though the Tartars have no right to Russian land, they in fact have "full civic equality." At this point we may recall Dostoevsky's argument, expounded elsewhere in *The Diary* (pp. 416 ff.), that land is the basis for human rights and that the European notion of abstract freedom for landless factory workers is a sham. Dostoevsky does not seem to be able to see

the Tartars as individuals, as human beings, undoubtedly because to do so would conflict with his idealization of the
Russians. The Tartars are a threat, an evil which must be
contained. They are an object to be defined, circumscribed,
and ruled by the Russian. No dialogue is possible with the
Tartar; he cannot become a subject. Finally, the denial of
subjectivity, of a voice, to the Tartar and the denial of his
right to land lead Dostoevsky to an openly political formulation of the relationship between the Russian and the Tartar.
The Russian is the "owner and master" (*vladitel' i khozjain*)
of the Russian land. Here the Russians are elevated to the
rank of landowners in relation to the Tartars (landless serfs).
In the light of this verbal subjugation, Dostoevsky's protestations of Russian tolerance and magnanimity toward the Muslims seem about as disinterested as British statements of civilizing intent in India or Africa.

The colonial comparison is not as gratuitous as it may
appear at first sight. In the last installment of *The Diary*
(January 1881) Dostoevsky returns to the question of the Russians' claim to lands occupied by Asiatic peoples. Elated by
General Skobelev's victory at Gheok Teppe, which sealed the
annexation of Turkestan, Dostoevsky unfolds his vision of
Russian expansion in Asia. Giving a new twist to his historio-
sophic scheme, he interprets Russian reluctance to realize the
importance of Asia as a consequence of Russia's two-hundred-year enslavement to Europe. Throughout the nineteenth century, he says, Russia has helped Europe to her own
detriment (*Diary*, pp. 1045–46). Now the time has come for a
regenerated Russia to turn eastward and take advantage of
the possibilities for her own aggrandizement.

Justifying Russia's mission in Asia to an imaginary Europeanized Russian who fears that a turn toward Asia will mean
stagnation, Dostoevsky says:

when we turn to Asia, with our new vision of her, in Russia there
may occur something akin to what happened in Europe when
America was discovered, since, in truth, to us Asia is like the then

undiscovered America. With our aspiration to become independent, we shall find out what to do, whereas during two centuries with Europe we lost the habit of any work; we became chatterers and idlers. . . . In Europe we were hangers-on and slaves, *whereas we shall go to Asia as masters. In Europe we were Asiatics, whereas in Asia we, too, are Europeans.* Our civilizing mission in Asia will bribe [*podkupit'*] our spirit and drive us there. It is only necessary that the movement should start. Build only two railroads: begin with the one to Siberia, and then to Central Asia—and at once you will see the consequences. [*Diary*, p. 1048; emphasis added]

In this passage, Dostoevsky has Russia, which considers herself inferior to Europe, turning to Asia and there assuming the European posture of domination and exploitation. Asia becomes the sphere in which Russia's identity is to be worked out in a travesty of Dostoevsky's beliefs about the organic, traditional values associated with the Russian peasant and the land. Dostoevsky now associates Russia's mission with her becoming a colonial power like the British in Africa. "Do you know that in Asia there are lands which are less explored than the interior of Africa?" (*Diary*, p. 1048). Here Dostoevsky becomes the advocate of capitalist expansion.[6] Russia should, he argues, exploit her vast hinterland as the English and Americans would know only too well how to do. "And do you know what riches are concealed in the bosom of these boundless lands? Oh, they [the English and Americans] would get at everything—metals, minerals, innumerable coal-fields; they would find and discover everything—and they would know how to use these minerals" (*Diary*, p. 1049). Asia will provide Russia with "experience," Dostoevsky says. Russians will be forced to become educated in science in order to exploit the resources of Asia. Again, as in his disenfranchisement of the Tartar, he asserts that the Russian claim to the land overrides that of the non-Russian inhabitants: "Wherever an 'Uruss' settles in Asia, the land will forthwith become Russian land" (*Diary*, p. 1050).

In the two passages discussed above, and indeed in all of his ideological writing, Dostoevsky seems caught in what

René Girard calls "the imitation of the other," of the rival.[7] Dostoevsky establishes rigid boundaries between the Russians and the others (Tartars, Asians, Europeans, Jews) in order to protect Russian autonomy. But the radical separation ends by distorting Russia's identity and forcing her to define herself in terms of the Other she has created. We are here at opposite poles from the fiction in which Dostoevsky exposes the mechanism of rejection and self-origination. In *Crime and Punishment*, Raskol'nikov's excesses are shown to follow from his extreme alienation from everything around him. In *The Diary*, Dostoevsky's opposition to Europe leads him to advocate political conquest as a means of fostering identity— the very idea which he denounced as the essence of European social thought, and which he attacked in his journalism and analyzed in the Grand Inquisitor chapter of *The Brothers Karamazov*.

These two passages, on the Tartars and on the Russian conquest of Asia, are only the most striking of the many pages in *The Diary* devoted to the central theme of Russia's impending awakening to a new national consciousness. Dostoevsky pursues this theme directly in the numerous articles in *The Diary* where he writes about the situation of the Slavs within the Turkish empire, the future of Constantinople, and the mission of Orthodox Russia. In all these articles, though less stridently than in the two passages above, Dostoevsky asserts Russia's uniqueness. Russia cannot be judged by the standards applied to other nations (*Diary*, p. 1033). Russia is above political interests (*Diary*, p. 556). One cannot help being struck by the fact that the same writer who in his fiction undercuts all notion of an absolute authority and reveals the interaction of different points of view[8] here lays claim to an absolute authority. Along with Russia's exemption from ordinary standards of judgment goes the tendency to blame the Other: Europe does not understand us (*Diary*, pp. 362, 556); Europe hates us (*Diary*, p. 295); Jews shun the company of

Russians (*Diary*, p. 644); Muslims avoid contact with Russians (*Diary*, p. 450).

What is surprising is that Dostoevsky ever breaks out of the ideological mode, or that the writer of the fiction still has the need to invoke the self-affirming judgments of the ideological mode. Given this contradiction, the two passages in *The Diary* in which Dostoevsky records his emergence from the ideological to the imaginative mode deserve special attention. As in the passages discussed above, we see Dostoevsky confronted with an opposition between self and other: between Russians and Jews in one case, and between the intellectual and the peasant in the other. Initially, Dostoevsky reacts defensively, by excluding, rejecting, blaming. But then he goes beyond rejection to a very different attitude of interest, understanding, and acceptance of what at first appeared foreign and threatening. Dostoevsky himself speaks of this new attitude in terms of artistic activity. It becomes clear that in telling of his change of heart he is also describing his access to the creative process.

The first of these passages appears in Dostoevsky's discussion of the "Jewish question" in *The Diary* (March 1877). He begins the article by responding to accusations of anti-Semitism made against him in a letter by an educated Jew. He proclaims his innocence of the charge, but in the course of defending himself, he unconsciously reveals his hostility and prejudice against the Jews. He admits to knowing very little about Jewish history, but asserts on the basis of his limited acquaintance with Jews (dating from his time in prison; *Diary*, p. 644) that they are all withdrawn, and look down on the Russians. He compares the suffering of the Jews to that of the Russians and concludes that surely they have not suffered more than the latter (*Diary*, p. 640-41). He asserts that Jews are driven by "their sempiternal pursuit of gold" (*Diary*, p.

641), that they have always exploited and allied themselves with those who exploited the defenseless Russian peasant (*Diary*, pp. 648–49), that they "have leaped *en masse* upon the millions of liberated Negroes and have already taken a grip upon them" (*Diary*, p. 642), and that they reign over the stock exchanges of Europe (*Diary*, p. 640). After all these charges, he asserts that the Russians have no a priori hatred of the Jew on religious grounds but only as a result of their persecution by the Jew. Finally, he makes the strange argument that all Jews, even those who are educated and profess atheism, believe secretly in Jehovah—that a Jew cannot be an atheist. This is a curious assertion for the creator of Kirillov. Dostoevsky here denies the Jew the same freedom which is in his view the "terrible burden" of the true Christian (*Diary*, p. 647).

In answering his correspondent's argument that the number of Jews who are actually in a position of economic dominance in Russia is extremely small and that the rest are in a state of poverty, Dostoevsky becomes incoherent. He admits that this may be the case but that it only proves that the others—those in dire poverty—have received a deserved retribution (*Diary*, p. 650).

For Dostoevsky, the Jew is by definition a threat to Russia's well-being; he represents something essential in the current disintegration of Russian society, in the loss of traditional values, the spread of atheism and materialism. There is some mystical correspondence between the Jew and the decay of Europe which Dostoevsky admits is not a question of numbers or of any monopoly of Jews in finance. Dostoevsky does not even see the necessity of explaining wherein this essence lies, though he concedes that most Jews are impoverished and that the Jews are not single-handedly responsible for the spiritual corruption of Europe (*Diary*, p. 650).

The early pages of this article show Dostoevsky intent on ascribing to a racial group the very traits which he analyzes in individual characters in the novels (the instinct to amass money, the impulse to withdraw from society), and the attribution of these traits to the Jew is mechanical, total, and final. Whereas in the case of Grushen'ka or Fedor Pavlovich, the instinct to amass money is shown to be a function of events in their pasts and is made comprehensible in terms of their individual psychologies, here—in the case of the Jew—the instinct to acquire money represents an essence; it is irreducible; it is not a function of anything else.

In all of this, it is clear to any reader, but not to Dostoevsky, that he sees the hostility between the Jews and the Russians to be the fault of the Jews alone, as a group, as a people with certain ineradicable traits (pursuit of gold, unwavering faith in their God, disdain for the Russian people, an instinct for merciless exploitation). At no point so far in his characterization does one feel that Dostoevsky sees Jews as individual people who exist in a concrete historical situation. He speaks of them in the same abstract, global way as he spoke of the Tartars[9] and "Asians." They are the Other, a threat, an enemy.

Again and again, Dostoevsky uses violent imagery to describe the behavior of the Jew: "what if the Jew, and his whole kehillah (vsem kagalom evrei) should fall upon the liberated peasant . . . ? . . . there would ensue such an era as could be compared not only with the era of serfdom but even with that of the Tartar yoke" (Diary, p. 651); "exterminate the rest, or make slaves of them, or exploit them" (Diary, p. 646; this is the Jews' program according to Dostoevsky); "how would it be if in Russia there were not three million Jews, but three million Russians, and there were eighty million Jews— well, into what would they convert the Russians and how would they treat them? . . . Wouldn't they convert them into slaves? Wouldn't they slaughter them to the last man, to the point of complete extermination, as they used to do with alien peoples in ancient times, during their ancient history?" (Diary, pp. 644-45). This recurrent insistence on violence without any reference to specific incidents or sources suggests projection on to the Jew of all that is viewed as evil or feared in oneself.

It seems that the circle of self-justification and accusation of the Other makes any resolution or deeper understanding of the "Jewish question" impossible. However, at this point, almost as an afterthought, Dostoevsky returns to the problem, but now in a markedly different vein. He begins to speak of a letter—this one from a Jewish girl—which he realizes "strangely fits into the whole chapter on the Jews which I have just finished writing. It might be too much to dwell again on the same subject, but this is a different theme, or even if it is the same theme, nevertheless it reveals the opposite aspect of the question, and even, as it were, a hint of its solution" (*Diary*, pp. 654-55). In the six-page postscript that follows we can see Dostoevsky the artist taking over from Dostoevsky the ideologist.

He proceeds to quote from the letter of the "young Jewish girl whom I know well" (*Diary*, p. 654) who writes to describe the funeral of a Dr. Hindenburg, who for fifty-eight years had treated the poor, including Jews, in the city of M. Rather than demanding payment, this doctor would delight in giving unexpected presents to his patients. A non-Jew, he was mourned at his funeral by Jews and non-Jews alike.

The girl's letter with its rather effusive description of the doctor's good deeds and the love for him shown at his funeral becomes the starting point for Dostoevsky's imagination. He conjures up a specific scene suggested by the letter: a Jewish woman in labor at dawn in her poor shanty, and the old doctor who has taken off his shirt to wrap the newborn baby in because the indigent Jews have no linen. Once having latched on to this "idea," Dostoevsky elaborates it with obvious enjoyment in the awareness that "With a refined feeling and intellect the artist may achieve much by the mere reshuffling of the roles of all these miserable household articles in a poor hut, and by this amusing reshuffle he can at once touch your heart" (*Diary*, p. 657). From a one-line mention of this incident in the letter (*Diary*, p. 655), Dostoevsky creates a verbal "painting" which takes up two pages. And this unpainted painting has what Dostoevsky finds lacking in the "pictures of some of our modern realists" (*Diary*, p. 657), that is, "a moral center." In this case, the vital "idea" of the picture is the gesture of the old doctor taking off his shirt in order to swathe the newborn Jewish baby. The realistic detail of the scene only achieves its significance in the light of this unique act captured in the imagined picture.

Dostoevsky unquestioningly accepts the girl's account (in contrast to the letter accusing him of anti-Semitism, which he rejects). He selects from it one particular image which strikes him and elaborates it, endowing it with its maximum resonance, significance of detail, and universality. The awareness that there is something of importance in the young girl's letter, something communicable, impels him to create the imaginary picture. He suggests, after his description of the scene, that "someone paint it" (*Diary*, p. 658) but we realize that he has already fixed the image indelibly in the reader's mind.

It is of the utmost importance to Dostoevsky's interpretation of the scene that the woman in labor be a Jew; and yet, there is nothing in Dostoevsky's description that distinguishes her and her family from other people. Dostoevsky refers to the woman in terms which unite her with all other women in labor: "Women subject to painful accouchement often bring forth the child at dawn: all night long they suffer great pains, and in the early morning they deliver the child" (*Diary*, p. 657). He refers to her as "the exhausted young woman in childbed looking at her newborn" (*Diary*, p. 658).

In the midst of his evocation of the scene, Dostoevsky exclaims:

Gentlemen, this is the solution of the Jewish question: the eighty-year-old naked torso of the doctor, shivering from the morning dampness, may assume a prominent place in the picture, not to speak of the face of the old man and that of the exhausted young woman in childbed looking at her newborn and the doctor's deeds. Christ sees all of this from above and the doctor knows this: "This poor Yiddisher will grow up, and, perhaps he himself will take his shirt off his shoulders and, remembering the story of his birth, will give it to a Christian." [*Diary*, p. 658]

Acts like the doctor's, though they may only be "isolated cases" (*Diary*, p. 659), provide an image of what is possible. They inspire legends and faith; "they constitute a living example, and, therefore, a proof" (*Diary*, p. 659). Dostoevsky shows how a particular event becomes transformed into a legend and into an image radiating outward beyond those immediately involved in it. The child may remember the story of the doctor's humanity later in his life and be affected by it. But even in the present, the doctor's funeral brings together all those who loved him, both Jews and non-Jews. The young girl who describes the funeral in her letter to Dostoevsky is preserving the memory of the doctor and propagating his act further outward from its center. Dostoevsky responds to her account and transforms it into an image which will reach even more readers.

The discovery of a resolution of the Jewish question—a resolution which is both moral and esthetic—coincides with the shift from a Manichean, abstract characterization of the Jews, which puts Dostoevsky firmly within the cycle of accusation and self-justification, to the evocation of a concrete scene in which Jews are portrayed as individual humans capable of eliciting a human response. Difference is acknowledged, but it is overcome by the recognition of a deeper identity.

The second passage in *The Diary* which records the shift from ideology to imagination appears in the issue of February 1876. Dostoevsky has been talking about the common people and the gentry's failure to see beneath their depravity and backwardness. After delineating his conditions for a reconciliation between the masses and the gentry, he proceeds to ask a question which occupies a central position in his thinking about Russia throughout his later writings: "Are our people predestined to pass through an additional phase of debauch and deceit, similar to that through which we passed when we were inoculated by civilization?" (*Diary*, p. 205). He confesses that he "would like to hear something more encouraging." In beginning the following section, he acknowledges that "all of these *professions de foi* must make very weary reading" (*Diary*, p. 205),[10] and he proposes to tell an anecdote. The anecdote is complex: it contains a memory from the age of nine surrounded by a scene remembered from Dostoevsky's term in the Omsk prison when he was twenty-nine—a memory within a memory. In prison, the vast majority of the convicts were illiterate peasants, and Dostoevsky, as an intellectual sentenced for a political offense, was painfully aware of the gulf between himself and his fellow prisoners. He begins the anecdote by describing the period of Easter Week in prison, when the convicts take advantage of their leisure to drink and quarrel:

Hideous, nasty songs; card-playing . . . ; several convicts, already beaten almost to death for disorderly conduct. . . . —all this in the course of the two-day holiday had exhausted me to the point of sickness. Never could I stand without disgust drunken popular rakishness, and particularly in this place. . . . Finally, anger arose in my heart: I met a Pole, M——tzki, a political criminal. He looked at me gloomily, his eyes flashing; his lips began to tremble: "Je hais ces brigands!" he told me in a low voice, grinding his teeth, and passed by. [*Diary*, p. 206]

In order to escape his oppressive surroundings, Dostoevsky goes to his bed and lies down on his back with his hands behind his head and with closed eyes (a position in which no one will disturb him) and tries, with difficulty, to let his mind wander. After a while, he reaches a state where he is freed from the painful impressions of the barracks and the sound of the Pole's words in his ears, and thoughts present themselves to him spontaneously:

By-and-by, I really forgot myself and became absorbed in reminiscences. Throughout my four years of hard labor I would constantly

reminisce about my past, and in my recollections I must have re-
lived my whole previous life. The recollections invaded my mind of
their own accord, and only on rare occasions did I evoke them by a
deliberate act of will. [*Diary*, p. 207]

As in the passage in which Dostoevsky describes the scene of
the Jewish mother after childbirth, he uses the metaphor of
painting to convey the process of making manifest what is
latent:

It used to begin with some speck, some trait—at times almost imperceptible—and then, gradually, it would grow into a complete
picture—some strong and solid impression. I used to analyze these
impressions, adding new touches to things long ago outlived, and—
what is more important—I used to correct, continually correct
them. Therein lay my whole diversion. On this occasion I suddenly
remembered one imperceptible moment in my early childhood,
when I was only nine years old—a moment which, so it seemed, was
altogether forgotten by me. [*Diary*, p. 207]

This memory presents itself to Dostoevsky at a moment
of alienation and sickness as something foreign to him, something from outside, like the Jewish girl's letter which acciden-
tally presents him with an image in which he sees the resolution of the "Jewish question." In both cases, he apprehends
the foreign thought as new, and this shift in vision, will allow
him to understand a present situation in new terms.

The memory is of his fright as a nine-year old when he
imagined hearing the cry of "Wolf!" and was comforted by
the old peasant Marei. Dostoevsky had forgotten about Marei and now, twenty years later, the incident presented itself
"distinctly, in every detail. This means that it had lodged in
my soul unnoticed, on its own, without any effort of my will,
and then came to my mind at the needed time" (*Diary*, p.
209). The memory of Marei's comforting the nine-year-old
child, like the imagined scene of the doctor swaddling the
Jewish baby, is accompanied by vivid, significant detail: "I
remembered particularly that thick finger of his, soiled with
earth, with which he so calmly, with such timid tenderness,
touched my trembling lip" (*Diary*, p. 209).

Dostoevsky then returns to the frame-memory and tells of the transforming effect of the childhood memory on his state of mind and on his view of the peasant convicts:

All of a sudden I awoke, seated myself on the sleeping boards and I remember, I still felt on my face the calm smile of reminiscence. . . . And when I climbed down off the boards and gazed around, I suddenly felt that I could behold these unfortunate men with a wholly different outlook, and suddenly, by some miracle, all the hatred and anger completely vanished from my heart. I went along, gazing attentively at the faces which I encountered. This drunken, shaven and branded peasant with marks on his face, bawling his hoarse, drunken song—why, he may be the very same Marei; for I have no way of peering into his heart. [*Diary*, pp. 209-10]

The seemingly bestialized peasants acquire a new freedom vis-à-vis Dostoevsky the observer. He suddenly realizes that he can have no idea of what underlies their repelling exterior. With the purging of resentment and hostility, the suffocating prison is transformed, and even the drunken, insensate Gazin (a Tartar, by the way) becomes a problem to be understood, a question that was not seen before. The transformation that Dostoevsky describes affects his attitude not only toward the peasants but even toward the educated Pole: "That same evening I met M——tzki once more. Unfortunate! Perhaps he could not have viewed these men differently than: 'Je hais ces brigands!' Yes, the Poles in these days had endured more than we!" (*Diary*, p. 210). This last sentence undoubtedly stands as the most sympathetic ever uttered by Dostoevsky about the Poles, or about most other nationalities, and contrasts markedly with his assertion that the Jews who complain so much about their suffering have not suffered as much as the Russian people. The Pole also presents Dostoevsky with an image of his own ideological side and his own hostility which Dostoevsky has just surmounted, but Dostoevsky apparently misses this irony.

In both cases discussed above, Dostoevsky describes an image or memory which extricates him from a difficult situation (the dilemma of the "Jewish question" and his discussion of the peasantry which he senses to be inadequate). Both cases involve the rescue of a child by an old man. The efficacy of this image, originating in the distant past, extends into the present for Dostoevsky. With its evocation, the feeling of disgust, suffocation, engulfment by his surroundings and the feeling of an insurmountable opposition between himself and others recede, and he is able to feel a new possibility of connectedness.

The shift from ideology—a closed, abstract, hostile view of the world based on irreconcilable differences—to an open, unguarded relation to the world in which detail becomes significant and helps to convey the importance of an event is accompanied by a new profusion of questions and answers, of significances. An abstract idea like the "Jew" or the "peasant" can take on associations and meaning which make it no longer refer to some foreign, undifferentiated group but to a tangible, universal human reality.

NOTES

Preface

1. I will use the terms "view of history" and "world view" interchangeably, though "world view" is a broader term. My assumption is that Dostoevsky expressed his world view primarily through his view of history.

2. It must be emphasized that the correspondence between the ideological and the journalism and between the imaginative and the fiction is approximate. There are certainly passages in the journalism in which Dostoevsky is self-critical, nondogmatic, and nonauthoritarian as well as moments of deep insight and moving experience. But they are, I think, exceptional. On the other hand, at certain points in the fiction Dostoevsky imposes his own viewpoint in a crude, absolutist way (most notably in Myshkin's tirade in *The Idiot* and in the portrayal of liberals, radicals and Poles in several of the novels). But, again, it is significant that these passages have a jarring effect and stand out as breaches of the novelist's detachment and comprehensive vision.

Chapter One. The Emancipation and the Intelligentsia

1. Tkachev, *Izbrannye sochinenija*, III, 219-20.

2. For a thorough and judicious account of Dostoevsky's involvement in the radical circles of the 1840's, see Frank, *Dostoevsky: The Seeds of Revolt*.

3. Robinson, *Rural Russia*, pp. 80, 88.

4. Kornilov, *Modern Russian History*, pp. 258-59.

5. Robinson, *Rural Russia*, pp. 87, 94.

6. Ibid., pp.104 ff.; Kornilov, *Modern Russian History*, p. 259.

7. Kochan, *Making of Modern Russia*, pp. 167, 169-170, 173-74; Robinson, *Rural Russia*, pp. 94-95, 111; Lampert, *Sons Against Fathers*, pp. 23, 25-26; Kornilov, *Modern Russian History*, p. 259.

8. Florinsky, *Russia*, II, 921; Kornilov, *Modern Russian History*, p. 264.

9. Emmons, *The Russian Landed Gentry and the Peasant Emancipation of 1861*, p. 421.

10. Ibid., p. 422.

11. Zaionchkovsky, "Capitalism and the 'Prussian Path' of Agrarian Development," in Emmons, ed., *Emancipation of the Russian Serfs*, pp. 104-5.

12. Kochan, *Making of Modern Russia*, p. 174.

13. Florinsky, *Russia*, II, 929.

14. Kochan, *Making of Modern Russia*, pp. 173-74.

15. The populists (*narodniki*) were a diverse group of intellectuals in the 1860s and 1870s (and later) united primarily by their concern for the situation of the Russian peasantry after the emancipation, their commitment to social justice and social equality, and their faith that Russia could avoid the ravages of capitalism by relying on her indigenous peasant institutions (above all, the commune). Within the broad spectrum of populism, many different positions were possible, ranging from the gradualist reformism of Lavrov to the Jacobinism of Tkachev and the "Buntarstvo" (the cult of mass rebellion) of Bakunin. Two indispensable studies of populism are Franco Venturi's *Roots of Revolution* and Andrzej Walicki's *The Controversy over Capitalism*.

16. Walicki, *The Controversy over Capitalism*, p. 24.

17. Ibid., p. 5.

18. Ibid., p. 12.

19. Ibid., p. 26.

20. It is true that Dostoevsky did not share the populists' enthusiasm for socialism and that he took great pains to distinguish his own Christian utopia from the socialist "antheap." But in spite of his open hostility to the idea of socialism in his last two decades, Dostoevsky's conception of the future society remained strongly influenced by the utopian socialism of his youth. Joseph Frank has suggested that, in his later years, Dostoevsky exaggerated the opposition between utopian socialism and Christianity for polemical purposes. Frank observes that the utopian socialism of the 1840s was actually permeated with Christian ideas. (See Frank's *Dostoevsky: The Seeds of Revolt*, pp. 184-95.) It appears that Dostoevsky's primary opponent in the 1860s and 1870s was not so much socialism itself as atheism (which he took to be an inseparable feature of socialism) and the repudi-

ation of ethics that accompanied the positivist-utilitarian version of social-ism popular in Russia in the 1860s.

21. This is not to say that Dostoevsky was influenced by the populists (most of whom were a good deal younger than he), but rather that he shared with them a common view of Russia's situation and of her future prospects, and that this view shaped his writings in crucial ways. The simi-larity of Dostoevsky's view of history to that of the populists is not surpris-ing when one realizes that the Slavophilism and utopian socialism of the 1840s left a strong imprint on both Dostoevsky and the populists. Populism could be characterized as a hybrid of Slavophilism and utopian socialism worked out by Herzen in reaction to the failure of the revolutions of 1848-49, and later developed by a new generation in the 1860s and 1870s as a response to the problematic situation in Russia following the emancipa-tion of the serfs.

Chapter Two. Period of Transition: Dostoevsky's View of History

1. *The Unpublished Dostoevsky*, II, 115.

2. References to *The Diary of a Writer* are to the English translation by Boris Brasol. In subsequent references, this work will be referred to as *Diary* and followed by a page number. Minor changes have been made in Brasol's translation where they seemed appropriate.

3. At one point in *The Diary*, Dostoevsky asks: "Besides, what true Russian doesn't think first about Europe?" (p. 250).

4. This doctrine, formulated by Dostoevsky and Apollon Grigorev, maintained that the alienation of the educated class—both Slavophiles and Westerners—stemmed from their detachment from the people and the "soil" (*pochva*) following Peter's reforms. The *pochvenniki* urged the intel-ligentsia to turn toward the common people and to seek national salvation in the principles of the "soil." Dostoevsky does not explicitly state what these principles are, but they seem to include Orthodoxy and the peasant's strong moral sense.

5. *The Notebooks for The Possessed*, p. 215.

6. Feuilleton of June 15, 1847, in *Chetyre stat'i 1847 g.*, p. 69.

7. *Intelligent* (a member of the intelligentsia) is used by Dostoevsky to refer to any member of the educated class in Russian society.

8. *Dostoevsky's Occasional Writings*, p. 246.

9. Ibid., p. 239.

10. The word "fantastic" is a key word in Dostoevsky's vocabulary. He applies it pejoratively to the Petersburg period and, as a term of distinction, to the literature which takes Russia's alienation as its subject.

11. Roman numerals in references refer to Dostoevskii, *Polnoe sobranie sochinenii v tridtsati tomakh* unless otherwise specified.

12. "Knizhnost' i gramotnost'," in *Dnevnik pisatelja*, I, 117.

13. In spite of his general concern for the peasantry, Dostoevsky never seems to have troubled himself about the niceties of *how much land* the peasants needed to subsist on or about the question of whether the peasants were economically better off before or after the emancipation, problems to which Chernyshevsky and others devoted enormous energies and which they felt to be decisive in evaluating the emancipation.

14. Manifesto for *Vremja* (October, 1862), in *Dostoevsky's Occasional Writings*, p. 247.

15. The *obshchina* was the traditional peasant commune in which land was periodically redistributed among the members and taxes were borne collectively. The *mir* was the peasants' assembly, which functioned as the executive organ of the *obshchina*. The *zemskii sobor* was the assembly of representatives of the different classes in the sixteenth and seventeenth centuries.

16. Walicki, *The Controversy over Capitalism*, p. 107.

17. Mikhailovskii, *Polnoe sobranie sochinenii*, 5th ed., I, 703.

18. Tkachev, *Izbrannye sochinenija*, II, 205.

19. Ibid., III, 69–70.

20. Ibid., II, 20.

21. Marx, *Early Writings*, p. 193.

22. Marx, *Capital*, I, 82n.

23. In what Venturi has called a "collective act of Rousseauism," in the summer of 1874 thousands of young men and women from the cities put on peasant clothes and went into the countryside to taste the simple, uncorrupted life of the people and to encourage them to rebel. The propaganda of these young intellectuals was met most often with incomprehension and suspicion from the peasants, who in many cases turned them over to the local authorities. See Venturi, *Roots of Revolution*, chapter 18.

24. From the first of two articles entitled "Knizhnost' i gramotnost'," published in *Vremja* (July 1861), reprinted in *Dnevnik pisatelja*, I, 118.

25. *Dnevnik pisatelja*, I, 100.

26. Ibid., p. 99.

27. Ibid., p. 42.

28. Ibid., p. 153.

29. Ibid., pp. 129–30.

30. *Vremja*, October 1861; in *Dostoevsky's Occasional Writings*, p. 240.

31. *Dnevnik pisatelja*, I, 115–16.

32. Herder actually contributed not only the form but also the content of Slavophilism: "He was convinced that the essential conditions for a good and civilized folk life were better fulfilled by the peaceful Slav peasant peoples than by the Germans, a proud warrior nation. Herder predicted for the Slavs a glorious future, and his sympathy for the Slav peoples, languages, and folkways was a powerful stimulant for the awakening of national consciousness among young Slav intellectuals at the beginning of the nineteenth century." Kohn, *Nationalism*, p. 32.

33. *Dostoevsky's Occasional Writings*, p. 239.

34. Ibid., p. 250.

35. Ibid., p. 246.

36. Ibid., p. 250.

37. Dostoevskii, *Polnoe sobranie sochinenii*, X, 198-99.

38. Minogue, *Nationalism*, pp. 25-26; Berlin, *Vico and Herder*, p. 180.

Chapter Three. The Imagination of Society

1. Dostoevskii, *Polnoe sobranie sochinenii v tridtsati tomakh*, IV, 9. All references are to this edition unless otherwise specified. The translations are mine.

2. The special division was reserved for the most hardened criminals. Dostoevsky says of them that they did not know the length of their sentences but considered themselves sentenced for life (IV, 11).

3. For a discussion of the narrator of the *Notes from the House of the Dead* in his conflicting roles as convict and memoirist and for Dostoevsky's attitude toward his prison experience, see Jackson, "The Narrator in Dostoevsky's *Notes from the House of the Dead*." Jackson concludes that "Dostoevsky resolved the potential contradiction between Goryanchikov the convict, unloving in his suffering, and Goryanchikov the memoirist, reconciled with the convicts and full of good will, by restricting Goryanchikov's memoirs to the first months, the first year in prison. Goryanchikov's broad and sympathetic view of the convicts, however, is actually based upon the experience of the 'later' years. Dostoevsky spent four terrible years in prison, but he condemned Goryanchikov to ten years: he gave him six more years to gain some perspective, to get over the 'first years' of hatred, horror and moral superiority before the convicts, to come to the conclusions which gradually ripened in Dostoevsky over the six years of his Siberian exile after his release from the prison at Omsk. It was necessary to present a narrator who, to some extent at least, practiced what he preached."

4. The description of A——v prefigures Svidrigailov on several points. A——v is a spy for the police; Svidrigailov spies on Raskol'nikov and threat-

ens to report him to the police. Both A——v and Svidrigailov are "lured by the temptations of Petersburg and its taverns" (IV, 62). In the *Notebooks for Crime and Punishment* Svidrgailov is called A——ov (see VII, 334 and IV, 285–86).

5. Apparently the comparison between prison life and life outside in favor of the former occurred to the censor also, who expressed the fear that chapter 2 of *Notes* made prison life look too attractive, since the convicts managed to obtain vodka and play cards and since the work was relatively light. The official of the Censorship Committee, expressing his apprehensions to the Main Censorship Bureau, wrote the following: "But taking account of the fact that, upon reading such an article, morally underdeveloped people who are restrained from crime by the severity of punishment alone, may, in spite of the direct sense of the article, take the humanitarian attitude of the government to mean that mild punishments are prescribed by law for serious crimes, the St. Petersburg Censorship Committee has the honor of presenting the aforementioned article for the approval of the Main Censorship Bureau, having marked those places which might have a perverting effect on undeveloped people." Dolinin, ed., *F. M. Dostoevskii, stat'i i materialy*, p. 361.

6. Blum, *Lord and Peasant in Russia*, p. 466.

7. The editors of *Polnoe sobranie sochinenii* [*Complete Collected Works*] comment in the Notes to *Notes from the House of the Dead*: "An analysis of the prison lists (*stateinye spiski*) allows us to draw general conclusions about the composition of the prisoners at the Omsk prison. The majority of them were peasants and soldiers (former peasants). Soldiers more often than peasants were sent to hard labor; the most common crimes were crimes against the military authorities and against the intolerable conditions of military service during the reign of Nicholas" (IV, 279–80).

8. Zherebjatnikov is an obvious predecessor of Fedor Pavlovich Karamazov. Both believe in birching. Both are passionately fond of playing perverse tricks on their victims. Both are likened to debauchees of the Roman empire (Fedor Pavlovich likes to boast of his Roman nose). They are both sentimental; Zherebjatnikov in a rhetorical sententia says, "I am a man, too," anticipating Fedor Pavlovich's justification of his behavior at the monastery. Furthermore, the convict whom he is about to have beaten cries out: "Be a father to me." Lastly, the tone of the passage just quoted resembles the tone in which the narrator of *The Brothers Karamazov* gives vent to his revulsion at Fedor Pavlovich.

9. In prison, Raskol'nikov will go through an evolution parallel to that of the narrator.The narrator refers to his state during his first years in prison as "*otchuzhdennost' i osobennost'*": alienation and peculiarity, words which also apply to Raskol'nikov.

10. The expectations of Dostoevsky upon his arrival at Omsk may to some degree have resembled those of the magnanimous official in "A Sordid Story" ("*Skvernyi anekdot*"), written apparently in the autumn of 1862. See *Polnoe sobranie sochinenii*, V, 352.

11. Turgenev, *Polnoe sobranie sochinenii i pisem*, IV, 319-20; Dostoevskii, *Polnoe sobranie sochinenii*, IV, 294.

12. See Nechaeva, *Zhurnal "Vremja,"* pp. 170-72. *Vremja* published Elizabeth Gaskell's novel *Mary Barton, A Story of Manchester Workers* in 1861 (issues 4-9), and *Sovremennik* published N. V. Shelgunov's "The Working Class in England and in France," also in 1861. Dolinin argues that Dostoevsky was profoundly influenced by Herzen's writings ("S togo berega" ["From the Other Shore"], "Pis'ma iz Frantsii i Italii" ["Letters from France and Italy"], and "Kontsy i nachala" ["Ends and Beginnings"]) both on the level of general ideas (such as the decadence of bourgeois Europe and Russia's role in reconciling the conflicting principles of society and the individual) and on the level of specific texts (Dolinin compares passages from "Pis'ma iz Frantsii i Italii" with passages from *Winter Notes*). See "Dostoevskii i Gertsen" in Dolinin, ed. *F. M. Dostoevskii, stat'i i materialy*, I, 275-324. Dostoevsky had visited Herzen during his brief stay in London.

13. Quoted by Marcus in *Engels, Manchester and the Working Class*, pp. 146-47.

14. Ibid., p. 209.

15. See the passage from *House of the Dead* quoted above, p. 64. "So perhaps a man buried alive and awakening in his coffin might beat on its lid and struggle to fling it off." The imagery also recalls the bath scene.

16. See *The Diary of a Writer*, p. 729.

17. Dostoevsky first identified the perfect society of the future with a prison in a passage which was left out of the final text of *Notes from the House of the Dead*. It reads, in part, as follows: "Try an experiment. Build a palace. Furnish it with statues, gold, heavenly birds, hanging gardens, with everything imaginable. . . . Go inside and perhaps you would never want to leave. And perhaps you really wouldn't ever leave. . . . But suddenly, a trifle! Your palace is surrounded by a fence and you are told: 'All of this is yours! Enjoy it! But don't set foot outside!' And rest assured that from that moment on you will want to give up your paradise and cross over the fence" (IV, 250).

18. Thirteen years later Dostoevsky would write in *The Diary of a Writer* in almost identical terms of the power of money in post-reform Russia; see *Diary*, pp. 486-87.

19. "*Voobshche burzhua ochen' ne glup, no u nego um kakoi-to koroten'kii, kak budto otryvkami*" (V, 85).

20. The image of the anthill as applied to human society seems to have been first used, in Russian, by Herzen, *Byloe i dumy*, III, 7. In English, the image is used by Wordsworth to describe London in *The Prelude*, Book VII, cited in Marcus, *Engels, Manchester, and the Working Class*, pp. 147–48.

21. Mochul'skii, *Dostoevskii*, p. 192.

22. Dostoevsky's description of Petersburg in *The Diary* ("Little Pictures," 1873) recalls his picture of London in several respects: the jarring contrast between wealth and poverty ("these wooden, rotten little houses still surviving, even in the most fashionable streets, side by side with enormous houses and suddenly striking one's eye as a heap of firewood near a marble palazzo"; *Diary*, p. 120); the dwarfing, imposing effect of large buildings and commercial enterprises ("And, finally, here we have the architecture of a modern, enormous hotel: this is a businesslike trend—Americanism, hundreds of rooms, a formidable industrial enterprise. One sees at once that we, too, have built railroads, and that all of a sudden we have become businessmen"; *Diary*, p. 121); the gloomy sight of workers (either drunk or with their "pale, emaciated, anemic" children) in the streets on Sundays (*Diary*, p. 122 ff.).

Chapter Four. The Economics of Writing

1. All quotations from the letters are from Dolinin, ed., *Pis'ma F. M. Dostoevskogo*, 4 vols. This edition will henceforth be referred to as *Pis'ma*. The translations are mine.

2. Cited in Jackson, *Dostoevsky's Quest for Form*, p. 160.

3. Many of the letters take the form of a detailed description of his predicament (his illness, lack of money, pressure of deadlines) culminating in a desperate plea for money which would "save" him.

4. Writing to Maikov from Geneva in August 1867, Dostoevsky remarks that "from a certain point of view" it would have been "very useful" for him to spend time in debtor's prison and that it was only owing to his recent marriage and the state of his health that he decided to escape his creditors by going to Europe (*Pis'ma*, II, 25–26).

5. Ortega y Gasset, *The Dehumanization of Art*, p. 180. In a letter to his brother Mikhail from prison in Omsk, Dostoevsky writes: "I will not tell you what has taken place in my soul, in my beliefs, in my mind and in my heart during these three years. It would take too long. But the continual concentration in myself, into which I escaped from a bitter reality, has yielded its fruits" (*Pis'ma*, I, 137).

6. *Pis'ma*, II, 14.

7. In the fall of 1865 too, Dostoevsky had lost all his money at roulette in Wiesbaden and had proposed to Katkov to write a story for *Russkii vestnik* about a young criminal. This story turned into *Crime and Punishment* (See *Pis'ma*, I, 415-21).

8. Freud in his essay "Dostoevsky and Parricide" links Dostoevsky's compulsion to lose at gambling to his need to be punished for having desired his father's death. Gambling is, for Freud, another symptom of Dostoevsky's neurosis like his epileptic fits. In Wellek, ed., *Dostoevsky*.

Chapter Five. Fantasy and Fiction

1. "The Dreamer of St. Petersburg," from Feuilleton of June 15, 1847, quoted in Terras, *The Young Dostoevsky*, pp. 313-16.

2. Jackson, *Dostoevsky's Quest for Form*, p. 167.

3. In Dostoevsky's last five novels, the fictional present coincides closely with the time of composition except for *The Brothers Karamazov* which, however, was presented by Dostoevsky as merely the prelude to the story of "the action of my hero in our day, *at the present time*" (emphasis added). The novels abound in references to recent events, such as the Franco-Prussian War and the Paris Commune in *The Possessed* and *A Raw Youth*, and the court reforms in *The Brothers Karamazov*.

4. *Polnoe sobranie sochinenii*, XIII, 455. The translations in this chapter are mine, unless otherwise specified.

5. In this connection, see the article "Anna Karenina as a Fact of Special Significance," in *The Diary* (p. 783 ff.).

6. One of the achievements of the later fiction is to emphasize the continuity of fantasy between the protagonist and the other characters. Fantasy proliferates to become the fundamental mode of being of almost all the characters, not just of a Goljadkin or a Prokharchin.

7. One might wonder why Raskol'nikov does not list Peter the Great among his great men, but then one realizes that none of Raskol'nikov's "extraordinary men" is Russian, and it is by his infatuation with *non-Russian* models that Raskol'nikov resembles Peter the Great. Raskol'nikov cites Lycurgus, Solon, Mohammed, and Napoleon.

8. The connection is made concretely in the figure of Fedor Pavlovich, who both abandons his children and despises the Russian people.

9. *Polnoe sobranie sochinenii*, V, 106.

10. Ibid., p. 104.

11. Ibid., pp. 108-9.

12. Ibid., X, 27.

13. R. D. Laing makes this point in *Self and Others*, pp. 65-66.

14. Svidrigailov is the most important fictional precursor of Fedor Pavlovich in *The Brothers Karamazov*. This is significant, above all, because in the relationship between Raskol'nikov and Svidrigailov we can already make out the father-son relationship and the issue of spiritual inheritance, what one generation has to pass on to the next. Svidrigailov is a "cynical father" like Fedor Pavlovich. His thoughts on an afterlife, his search for solidity in debauchery, defilement, his mocking of romanticism ("Schiller"), his use of French, his reference to *"Homo sum et nihil humanum a me alienum puto"* —all anticipate Fedor Pavlovich.

15. In his discussion of Raskol'nikov, Georg Lukács says: "Dostoevsky's characters go to the end of the socially necessary self-destruction unafraid, and their self-dissolution, their self-execution, is the most violent protest that could have been made against the organization of life in that time." Wellek, ed., *Dostoevsky*, p. 156. Lukács' essay is suggestive in spite of his rather forced conclusion that Raskol'nikov's revolt is "historically progressive."

16. *The Notebooks for Crime and Punishment*, p. 64.

17. Girard, *Dostoievski*, pp. 89 ff.

18. Letter to Strakhov from October 9/21, 1870: "In a word, never has any work cost me so much work" (*Pis'ma*, II, 294).

19. Letter to his niece, from August 17/29, 1870 (*Pis'ma*, II, 283).

20. This, of course, anticipates Ivan's question to Alesha: "Imagine that you are creating a fabric of human destiny with the object of making men happy in the end, giving them peace and rest at last, but that it is essential and inevitable to torture to death only one tiny creature—that baby beating its breast with its fist, for instance—and to found that edifice on its unavenged tears. Would you consent to be the architect on those terms?" *Sobranie sochinenii*, IX, 308.

21 Miller, *Poets of Reality*, p. 41.

22. See Girard's discussion of the mechanism of snobbism, dissimulation, and "metaphysical desire" in *Mensonge romantique et vérité romanesque*.

23. *The Notebooks for The Possessed*, p. 244.

24. Ibid., p. 219; pp. 147, 238, 253.

25. Ibid., p. 366.

26. Ibid., pp. 155, 130.

27. Ibid., pp. 163, 225, 357, 373, 418.

28. Ibid., pp. 236-37.

29. Ibid., p. 237.

30. Ibid., p. 236.

31. Said, "Narrative," p. 71.

32. All references to *The Brothers Karamazov* are to F. M. Dostoevskii, *Sobranie sochinenii*, IX-X.

33. The characterization of Fedor Pavlovich as a tavernkeeper and a moneylender (IX, 31), and his association with Jews (IX, 31), connect him with Dostoevsky's fears that the Russian peasant and the commune are being ruined by kulaks, merchants and vodka. For a typical expression of these fears, see *The Diary*, pp. 105-6. It is significant, however, that, given these underlying associations, Fedor Pavlovich is not just a symbol or a caricature, but a complex and even sympathetic character.

34. The basic ideas and imagery contained in "The Grand Inquisitor" were given expression as early as *Winter Notes* and in the notes for the unfinished article "Socialism and Christianity" which Dostoevsky worked on in 1864-65. See *Neizdannyi Dostoevskii*, p. 39; *The Unpublished Dostoevsky*, pp. 95-98.

35. For an exception to this rule, see Belknap, *The Structure of the Brothers Karamazov*. Belknap argues for the connectedness of "The Grand Inquisitor" with the rest of the novel, pp. 64-65. His study as a whole emphasizes the technical means by which Dostoevsky achieved complexity and coherence in *The Brothers Karamazov*.

36. *Polnoe sobranie sochinenii*, V, 69; I. I. Lapshin points to the description of London in *Winter Notes* as a source of the Grand Inquisitor in his article "Kak slozhilas' Legenda o Velikom Inkvisitore," in Bem, ed., *O Dostoevskom*, pp. 138-39.

37. Belknap has pointed out the association between Fedor Pavlovich and the devil via the common element of buffoonery. See *The Structure of The Brothers Karamazov*, pp. 41-45. No one, to my knowledge, has called attention to the implications of this association for an understanding of Ivan.

38. This sentence also links Fedor Pavlovich to the devil through Svidrigailov who, as we have noted, is a predecessor of Fedor Pavlovich and who says in *Crime and Punishment*: "I, too, am a man, *et nihil humanum* . . ." *Polnoe sobranie sochinenii*, VI, 215.

39. Freud, *Totem and Taboo*, p. 72.

Chapter Six Creative Process: From Ideology to Imagination

1. Yarmolinsky, "Dostoievsky: A Study in His Ideology," pp. 63-64.
2. Bakhtin, *Problems of Dostoevsky's Poetics*, trans. Rotsel, pp. 55-56.
3. I have in mind the motif of relatedness in the novels. Characters continually try to convince one another that they have something in common in spite of appearances to the contrary (e.g., Svidrigailov-Raskol'nikov, Raskol'nikov-Sonja, Smerdjakov-Ivan, Dmitrii-Alesha).

4. This ambiguity of the author's relation to his characters has prompted biographers and critics to speculate about Dostoevsky's attitude toward such complex characters as Stavrogin and Ivan. There is little such ambiguity in *The Diary of a Writer*.

5. All page references to *The Diary of a Writer* are to Brasol's translation.

6. This is the capitalist expansion that Lebedev in *The Idiot* (1868) paints in apocalyptic terms which go back to Dostoevsky's vision of London described in *Winter Notes* (1863).

7. Girard, *Mensonge romantique et vérité romanesque*, p. 12 ff.

8. Bakhtin, *Problems of Dostoevsky's Poetics*, pp. 14, 64, 66.

9. This equivalence of the Tartars and Jews as enemies which must be dislodged and kept at a distance is made explicit in a passage in *The Diary* where Dostoevsky endorses the idea of evicting the Tartars from the Crimea (their home for four hundred years) on the grounds that the Russians would make better use of the land. He concludes: "In any event, should the Russians fail to settle in the Crimea, the Jews without fail would fall upon her [the Crimea] and exhaust her soil" (*Diary*, p. 370).

10. Note the parallel to his fear of boring the reader by prolonging his discussion of the Jewish question (*Diary*, p. 655).

BIBLIOGRAPHY

Bakhtin, M. M. *Problemy poetiki Dostoevskogo.* Moscow: Sovetskii Pisatel', 1963; *Problems of Dostoevsky's Poetics,* trans. R. W. Rotsel. Ann Arbor: Ardis, 1973.

Belknap, Robert L. "Dostoevsky's Nationalist Ideology and Rhetoric." In *Russia: The Spirit of Nationalism,* ed. Charles A. Moser. *Review of National Literatures,* 3, no. 1 (Spring 1972), 89-100.

——"The Origins of Alesha Karamazov." In *American Contributions to the Sixth International Congress of Slavists, Prague, 1968,* vol II, *Literary Contributions,* ed. William E. Harkins. The Hague: Mouton, 1968, pp. 1-21.

——"The Sources of Mitja Karamazov." In *American Contributions to the Seventh International Congress of Slavists, Warsaw, 1973,* vol. II, *Literature and Folklore,* ed. Victor Terras. The Hague: Mouton, 1973, pp. 39-51.

——*The Structure of The Brothers Karamazov.* The Hague: Mouton, 1967.

Bem, A. L. *O Dostoevskom, sbornik statei.* [On Dostoevskii, A Collection of Articles.] Ann Arbor: University Microfilms, 1963. 3 vols.

——*Dostoevskii, psikhoanaliticheskie etjudy.* [Dostoevsky, Psychoanalytic Studies.] Ann Arbor: University Microfilms, 1963.

Berlin, Isaiah. *Vico and Herder: Two Studies in the History of Ideas.* New York: Vintage Books, 1977.

Billington, James. *Mikhailovsky and Russian Populism.* New York: Oxford University Press, 1958.

194   BIBLIOGRAPHY

Blum, Jerome. *Lord and Peasant in Russia from the Ninth to Nineteenth Century.* Princeton: Princeton University Press, 1961.

Borshchevskii, S. *Shchedrin i Dostoevskii.* [Shchedrin and Dostoevsky.] Moscow: Gosudarstvennoe Izdatel'stvo Khudozhestvennoi Literatury, 1956.

Carr, E. H. *Michael Bakunin.* New York: Vintage Books, 1937.

Dolinin, A. S. *Poslednie romany Dostoevskogo.* [Dostoevsky's Last Novels.] Moscow: Sovetskii Pisatel', 1963.

——*V tvorcheskoi laboratorii Dostoevskogo.* [In Dostoevsky's Creative Laboratory.] Moscow: Sovetskii Pisatel', 1947.

——, ed. *F. M. Dostoevskii, stat'i i materialy.* [F. M. Dostoevsky, Articles and Materials.] Petersburg: Mysl, 1922-24, 2 vols.

——, ed. *Pis'ma F. M. Dostoevskogo.* [The Letters of F. M. Dostoevsky.] Moscow: Gosudarstvennoe Izdatel'stvo, 1928-59, 4 vols.

Dostoevskii, F. M. *Chetyre stat'i 1847 g.* [Four Articles from 1847.] Introduction by V. S. Nechaeva. Petersburg and Berlin: Epokha, 1922.

——*The Diary of a Writer,* trans. Boris Brasol. New York: George Braziller, 1954.

——*Dnevnik pisatelja.* [The Diary of a Writer.] Paris: YMCA Press, n.d., 3 vols.

——*Dostoevsky's Occasional Writings,* ed. and trans. David Magarshack. New York: Random House, 1963.

——*Neizdannyi Dostoevskii.* [The Unpublished Dostoevsky.] *Literaturnoe nasledstvo.* Vol. 83. Moscow: Nauka, 1971.

——*The Notebooks for Crime and Punishment,* ed. and trans. Edward Wasiolek. Chicago: University of Chicago Press, 1967.

——*The Notebooks for The Possessed,* ed. Edward Wasiolek, trans. Victor Terras. Chicago: University of Chicago Press, 1968.

——*Polnoe sobranie sochinenii v tridtsati tomakh.* [Complete Collected Works in Thirty Volumes.] Vols. I-XI. Leningrad: Nauka, 1972-74.

——*Sobranie sochinenii v desjati tomakh.* [Collected Works in Ten Volumes.] Vols. IX-X. Moscow: Gosudarstvennoe Izdatel'stvo Khudozhestvennoi Literatury, 1957-58.

——*The Unpublished Dostoevsky.* General ed. Carl R. Proffer. Vols. I and II. Ann Arbor: Ardis, 1973-75.

Emmons, Terence, ed. *Emancipation of the Russian Serfs.* New York: Holt, Rinehart, and Winston, 1970.

——*The Russian Landed Gentry and the Peasant Emancipation of 1861.* London: Cambridge University Press, 1968.

Fanger, Donald. *Dostoevsky and Romantic Realism.* Canbridge, Mass.: Harvard University Press, 1965.

Florinsky, Michael T. *Russia: A History and Interpretation.* Vol. II. New York: Macmillan, 1947.

Frank, Joseph. "Dostoevsky and Russian Nihilism: A Context for *Notes from Underground.*" Ph.D. diss., University of Chicago, 1960.

——*Dostoevsky: The Seeds of Revolt, 1821-1849.* Princeton: Princeton University Press, 1976.

——"The House of the Dead." *The Sewanee Review,* 74 (Autumn 1966), 779-803.

——"The Masks of Stavrogin." *The Sewanee Review,* 77 (Autumn 1969), 660-91.

——"Nihilism and *Notes from Underground.*" *The Sewanee Review,* 69 (Winter 1961), 1-33.

——"The World of Raskol'nikov." *Encounter,* June 1966.

Freud, Sigmund. "Dostoevsky and Parricide." In *Dostoevsky: A Collection of Critical Essays,* ed. René Wellek. Englewood Cliffs, N.J.: Prentice-Hall, 1962.

——*Totem and Taboo.* New York: Norton, 1950.

Gerstein, Linda. *Nikolai Strakhov.* Cambridge, Mass.: Harvard University Press, 1971.

Gide, André. *Dostoevsky.* Introduction by Arnold Bennett. New York: New Directions, 1961.

Girard, René. *Dostoievski: du double à l'unité.* Paris: Plon, 1963.

——*Mensonge romantique et vérité romanesque.* Paris: Grasset, 1961.

Goldmann, Lucien. *Le dieu caché.* Paris: Editions Gallimard, 1959.

——*Pour une sociologie du roman.* Paris: Editions Gallimard, 1964.

Grossman, L. *Dostoevskii, put', poetika, tvorchestvo.* [Dostoevsky, His Life, Poetics, and Works.] Moscow: Sovremennye Problemy, 1928.

Herzen, A. I. *Byloe i dumy.* [My Past and Thoughts.] Moscow: Khudozhestvennaja Literatura, 1967. 3 vols.

Jackson, Robert L. *Dostoevsky's Quest for Form: A Study of His Philosophy of Art.* New Haven: Yale University Press, 1966.

——"The Narrator in Dostoevsky's *Notes from the House of the Dead.*" In *Studies in Russian and Polish Literature. In Honor of Waclaw Lednicki,* ed. Zbigniew Folejewski. The Hague: Mouton, 1962.

Kochan, Lionel. *The Making of Modern Russia.* Middlesex, England: Penguin Books, 1963.

Kohn, Hans. *Nationalism: Its Meaning and History,* rev. ed. Princeton: Van Nostrand, 1955.

——*Prophets and Peoples: Studies in Nineteenth Century Nationalism.* New York: Macmillan, 1952.

Kornilov, Alexander. *Modern Russian History: Nineteenth Century Russia from the Age of Napoleon to the Eve of Revolution,* A. S. Kaun, ed. and trans; abridged by Robert Bass. New York: Capricorn Books, 1966.

Laing, R. D. *Self and Others.* Middlesex, England: Penguin Books, 1971.

Lampert, E. *Sons Against Fathers.* London: Oxford University Press, 1965.

Lapshin, I. I. *Estetika Dostoevskogo.* [Dostoevsky's Esthetics.] Berlin: Obelisk, 1923.

Lukács, Georg. "Dostoevsky." In René Wellek, ed., *Dostoevsky: A Collection of Critical Essays.* Englewood Cliffs, N.J.: Prentice-Hall, 1962, pp. 146-58.

Malia, Martin. *Alexander Herzen and the Birth of Russian Socialism, 1812-1855.* Cambridge, Mass,: Harvard University Press, 1961.

——"What Is the Intelligentsia?" In Richard Pipes, ed. *The Russian Intelligentsia.* New York: Columbia University Press, 1961.

Marcus, Steven. *Engels, Manchester and the Working Class.* New York: Vintage Books, 1974.

Marx, Karl. *Capital: A Critique of Political Economy,* ed. Frederick Engels. Vol. I. New York: International Publishers, 1967.

——*Early Writings,* ed. and trans. T. B. Bottomore. New York: McGraw-Hill, 1964.

Matlaw, Ralph E. *The Brothers Karamazov: Novelistic Technique.* The Hague: Mouton, 1957.

Mikhailovskii, N. K. *Polnoe sobranie sochinenii.* [Complete Collected Works.] 5th ed. Vol. I. St. Petersburg: Russkoe Bogatstvo, 1911.

Miller, J. Hillis. *Poets of Reality.* Cambridge, Mass.: Belknap Press of Harvard University Press, 1965.

Minogue, K. R. *Nationalism.* Baltimore: Penguin Books, 1970.

Mochul'skii, Konstantin. *Dostoevskii: zhizn i tvorchestvo.* [Dostoevsky: His Life and Work.] Paris: YMCA Press, 1947.

Nechaeva, V. S. *Zhurnal M. M. i F. M. Dostoevskikh "Vremja," 1861-1863.* [M. M. and F. M. Dostoevsky's Journal "Vremja," 1861-1863.] Moscow: Nauka, 1972.

Nejfel'd, Jolan. *Dostoevskii, psikhoanaliticheskii ocherk.* [Dostoevsky, A Psychoanalytic Sketch.] Leningrad: Petrograd, 1925.

Ortega y Gasset, José. *The Dehumanization of Art and Other Writings on Art and Culture.* Garden City, N. Y.: Anchor Books, 1956.

Pereverzev, V. F. *F. M. Dostoevskii.* Moscow: Gosudarstvennoe Izdatel'stvo, 1925.

Riasanovsky, Nicholas V. *Nicholas I and Official Nationality in Russia, 1825-55.* Berkeley and Los Angeles: University of California Press, 1959.

Robinson, Geroid Tanquary. *Rural Russia under the Old Regime.* Berkeley and Los Angeles: University of California Press, 1969.

Said, Edward W. "Narrative: Quest for Origins and Discovery of the Mausoleum." *Salmagundi,* 12 (Spring 1970), 63-75.

Sandoz, Ellis. *Political Apocalypse: A Study of Dostoevsky's Grand Inquisitor.* Baton Rouge: Louisana State University Press, 1971.

Schapiro, Leonard. *Rationalism and Nationalism in Russian Nineteenth-Century Political Thought.* New Haven: Yale University Press, 1967.

Simmons, Ernest J. *Dostoevsky: The Making of a Novelist.* New York: Random House, 1940.

Terras, Victor. *The Young Dostoevsky (1846-1849): A Critical Study.* The Hague: Mouton, 1969.

Tkachev, P. N. *Izbrannye sochinenija.* [Selected Works.] Moscow:

Izdatel'stvo Vsesojuznogo Obshchestva Politkatorzhan i Ssyl'-no-Pocelentsev, 1932–33. Vols. II and III.

Turgenev, I. S. *Polnoe sobranie sochinenii i pisem.* [Complete Collected Works and Letters.] Moscow and Leningrad: Izdatel'stvo Akademii Nauk SSSR, 1962. Vol. IV.

Venturi, Franco. *The Roots of Revolution: A History of the Populist and Socialist Movements in Nineteenth Century Russia.* Introduction by Isaiah Berlin. New York: Grosset and Dunlap, 1960.

Vucinich, Wayne S., ed. *The Peasant in Nineteenth-Century Russia.* Stanford: Stanford University Press, 1968.

Walicki, Andrzej. *The Controversy over Capitalism.* London: Oxford University Press, 1969.

——*The Slavophile Controversy: History of a Conservative Utopia in Nineteenth-Century Russian Thought,* trans. Hilda Andrew-Rusiecka. London: Oxford University Press, 1975.

Wellek, René, ed. *Dostoevsky: A Collection of Critical Essays.* Englewood Cliffs, N.J.: Prentice-Hall, 1962.

——*A History of Modern Criticism: 1750–1950.* New Haven: Yale University Press, 1965. Vol. III.

Wortman, Richard. *The Crisis of Russian Populism.* London: Cambridge University Press, 1967.

Yarmolinsky, Avrahm. *"Dostoievsky: A Study in His Ideology."* PhD. diss., Columbia University, 1921.

INDEX

Alexander II, 1, 9, 28
Anti-Semitism, ix, 163, 171–76
Asia, Russia's mission in, 50, 168–70

Bakunin, Mikhail, 6
Brothers Karamazov, The, 142–62, 164, 170; and The Diary of a Writer, 142–44; theme of denial of relationship in, 144–46, 154–55, 158–62; "Rebellion" chapter in, 147–49; Ivan and the "Grand Inquisitor," 126, 149–54; and Winter Notes, 151, 191n36; and Notes from the House of the Dead, 158

Capital (Marx), 7
Capitalism, 4–7; and socialism, 80–81
Chernyshevsky, N. G., 4, 81, 184n13
Commune (obshchina), 2, 4, 6–7, 30, 32–34, 38, 184n15
Community, sense of, 18, 20, 30, 31, 136, 162; lack of in Europe, 23–27, 76–86
Condition of the Working Class in England in 1844 (Engels), 78
Crime and Punishment, 59, 75, 120–31, 170; theme of the intolerable present in, 122; image of a golden age in, 129
Culture, 14–16, 41–46

Dead Souls (Gogol), 136
Diary of a Writer, The, vii, 113, 118, 142–44, 164–79; post-emancipation period, 10; alienation of intelligentsia as the central theme of, 15–22; Europe, 22–30; the people, 30–33, 41–42; money, 35–39
Dickens, Charles, 34
Dolinin, A. S., 187n12

Doré, Gustave, 34
Dostoevsky, Fedor Mikhailovich: world view, vii, ix, 11; relation to populism, 5, 7–8, 32–35, 182n20, 183n21; on emancipation, 9–10; on post-reform period, 10–11; on Europe, 14, 22–30, 187n12; use of word "fantastic," 21, 116, 183n10; on Christ, 23–24; on Catholicism, 23–24, 27; on socialism, 24, 80–81, 85–86, 125–26, 187n17; on the people, 30–33, 176–80; on crime, 31; belief in "privilege of backwardness," 31–33; fears about Russia's future, 33–34, 39; on money, 35–39; on the people and the intelligentsia, 40–42; on literacy and literature, 43–44; on nationality, 46–47; nationalism, 49–51, 167–69; imprisonment, 54 (see also Notes from the House of the Dead); on his situation as a writer (in letters), 93–110; gambling, 96–100; writing as gambling, 100–2; conflict between external pressures and demands of literary creation, 101–4; on aristocratic literature, 104–6; claim to originality, 106–10; on realism, 108–9

"Eighteenth Brumaire of Louis Bonaparte, The" (Marx), 25
Emancipation of the serfs, 1, 9–10, 30, 37–38; effect on the peasantry, 2–3; effect on the gentry, 3–4; as a spur to capitalism, 4; as a landmark, 5–6
Emmons, Terence, 3
Engels, Friedrich, 76–79
Epokha, vii
Eternal Husband, The, 105
Europe, 13–14, 22–30

Fantasy, ix, 21, 96–100, 112, 114–20, 123–27, 130–31, 133, 136–40, 146–49, 158, 162, 189n6
Fiction, 111–62; relation to other writings, 39, 90–91, 111–13; dominant patterns in, 114–20; theme of abandonment in, 117–20
Flerovsky, V. V. (Bervi), 6, 34
Fourier, Charles, 54
France: the Third Republic in, 25–27
Freud, Sigmund, 162, 189n8

Gambler, The, 113
Gambling, ix, 96–100
Gaskell, Elizabeth, 34
"Gentle Creature, A," 113
Girard, René, 137, 170
Goncharov, I. A., 105
Grigorovich, D. V., 107

Hegel, G.W.F., 49
Herder, J. G., 46, 49, 185n32
Herzen, A. I., 4, 183n21, 187n12, 188n20

Ideological mode, ix; contrasted with imaginative mode, 11–13, 51, 75, 149–50, 163–66; as a defense, 170; shift from ideological to imaginative mode, 111–12, 174–76, 179–80
Idiot, The, 100–4, 131–32
Imaginative mode, ix, 12, 111–12, 174–76, 179–80, 181n2
Intelligent, 16, 112, 114–18
Intelligentsia, 1, 6–8, 14–22; desire to merge with the people, 40–42, 184n23; contempt for the people, 18–19

Jackson, Robert, 111
Jews, 171–76
Journalism, viii, 9–51, 111–13, 115, 163–80

Katkov, Mikhail, 95, 99
Kochan, Lionel, 5

Lavrov, P. L., 6, 14
Letters, of Dostoevsky, 93–110, 112, 113

Marx, Karl, 25, 26, 50; on money, 37–38
Mikhailovsky, N. K., 6, 14, 32, 34, 90
Miller, J. Hillis, 136
Mochul'skii, Konstantin, 88

Narodnichestvo, see Populism; Populists
Nationalism, 49–51, 166–71
Nationality, principle of, 46–49
National spirit (Volksgeist), 44–45, 47
Nechaev, S. G., 47
Nicholas I, 1
Notebooks to Crime and Punishment, 131
Notebooks to The Possessed, 132, 138–41
Notes from the House of the Dead, 53–74, 111; peasant convicts and educated convicts, 55; raises questions about Russian society, 57, 61–68; narrator and Dostoevsky, 57, 71–72, 185n3; punishment, 61–68; plea for humane treatment of convicts, 69–70
Notes from Underground, 80, 81, 113, 165

Obshchina, see Commune
Ortega y Gasset, José, 96

Peasantry, situation of, 2–3, 5, 10
"Pedantry and Literacy," 40, 42
Peter the Great, 13–15, 45
Petersburg, 21–22, 90, 120, 188n22
"Petersburg period," 10, 13–15, 22, 44, 45, 49, 51, 113, 115–19, 129, 142
Petrashevsky circle, 54
Pochvennichestvo (doctrine of the soil), 14, 49, 74, 89, 183n4
Pomjalovsky, N. G., 109
Populism: hallmarks of, 7
Populists, 6–9, 90, 182n15; fear of capitalist development, 31–34; and doctrine of the national spirit, 47
Possessed, The, 25, 48, 103, 131–42; theme of contradiction in, 132–37; theme of inheritance in, 138–42
Post-emancipation period, contradictions of, 4–5, 10, 18
Pushkin, 44–46

Raw Youth, A, 113–14, 118, 143
Raznochintsy, 109

Reshetnikov, F. M., 109
Russia: in relation to Europe, 13–14, 22, 25, 28–30, 32, 74, 141; Petersburg as symbol of, 22; and the people, 30–33

Said, Edward, 142
Schlegel, Friedrich, 46–47
Serfdom, and alienation of the intelligentsia, 14–15
Slavophiles, 4, 38, 47
Sleptsov, V. A., 109
Socialism, 24, 80–81, 85–86, 125–26, 187n17
Society: criticism of, 8; Petersburg as image of, 21, 188n22; European society, 22–23, 75–91; exclusion of criminal from, 31, 67, 158–62; and prison, 62–67; the perfect society as a prison, 80–81, 187n17; alternative forms of, 85–88; as an anthill, 86; 188n20; transformation of, 35, 116, 119, 125, 130–31, 136, 149, 151–52, 158

Tartars, 166–68, 192n9
Tkachev, P. N., 6, 34–35, 47
Tolstoy, Lev, 46, 105
"To the People" Movement, 40, 184n23
Turgenev, Ivan, 73, 105

Underground Man, the, 117–18
Uspensky, G. I., 109
Utopian socialism, 1, 54, 182n20; see also Socialism

Volk, 47
Volksgeist, 47
Vremja, viii, 40, 74, 187n12

Walicki, Andrzej, 7–8, 31
Westerners, 47
Winter Notes on Summer Impressions, 21, 74–91, 111; raises questions about Russian society, 75; and House of the Dead, 75, 79–80; reaction to London in, 76–82; reaction to Paris in, 81–84; criticism of socialism, 85–86; Dostoevsky's social ideal, 87–88; concern for Russia's future, 89–91
World view (view of history), vii–ix, 11, 15, 51
Writing: as mediation, 11, 96–97, 119–20

Xenophobia, 167–70, 192n9

Zaionchkovsky, P. A., 4